Cracking the Kindle Sales Code

*How To Search Engine Optimize Your Book So
Amazon Promotes and Recommends it To Everyone*

by **Dr. Robert C. Worstell**

Table of Contents

Bonus

Get Related Writing and Publishing Materials From Our Free Library

Instant Access – Join Here

Click or type into your browser:

http://livesensical.com/go/writingbooks/

Before You Begin

If you're here just to learn about more tips and tricks for Search Engine Optimization (SEO) then start at Chapter 2.

If you want to learn how SEO fits into helping any indie author earn more income from their books, keep reading from here.

Either way, enjoy your journey.

Why Most Authors Can Only <u>Hope</u> Their Book Sells on Amazon?

1.1. Kindle Has a Success Code You Can Crack

Unsuccessful authors stay ignorant and broke.
Successful authors have discovered and use a simple formula to make their success on Kindle.

True financial freedom is possible from book sales. You or anyone you know could get there.

Then why do only a few *really* get there?

Book sales is a game. It runs on code. It can be won. But first, like any game, you have to know the rules. Most self-publishers don't know all the rules, or even most of them.

Unfortunately most of available self-publishing advice and courses either don't have the full scene, or they only deal with a small part. (And the truly bad ones just want your money to get you published at all.)

The biggest hole to fall into is after the book is published. Most authors run on "hope publishing." This is where you publish the book, tell everyone you know it's up there, and then hope for the best. Obviously, this isn't going to be anything you can count on for income. There is no magic wand which will turn any single book into a bestseller.

This shortish introduction is here to connect the dots and give a rough outline and overview of steps so you can then know what you need to do. And then you'll know where you're missing data and can find the books and courses which cover these steps. Several resources are listed in the Appendix to help you with this.

Once the writer has his books ready to publish, the author probably then asks:

1. How do I get my books to sell and earn income?

2. How much is it going to cost me?

The basic problem all self-publishing authors have is that they don't know what they don't know. And so they don't know where to look to find what they need to know.

But in order to succeed, you need to study the successful...

Where the 6-figure Authors Get Their Income

What follows is based on continual study over a decade of the successful authors, even if they are accidentally successful (and their peak in income is temporary.) Any success is exceptional, and what they did to achieve it isn't what most authors are doing and usually is known by only a handful out of millions.

By several surveys, the average author publishes one book, makes about $500 per year, and will sell about 100-250 copies of that book total.

In studying successful authors you find:

- a 6-figure annual income is common
- While this dwindles over time, it continues in 5- or 6-figure incomes for the data we have.
- They start out with 6-10 books (in series) immediately, or within the first two years.
- They publish in all possible formats and versions, usually through all possible outlets.

Why do they succeed?

- *Multiple eyeballs* can find their work in the format they want, wherever they are looking.
- A *deep backbench* of books means people are looking for a earlier books in that series when they read a later one.

- (and other reasons, we'll get to.)

Do authors who just write and publish 6-10 books succeed? Not usually. Not enough eyeballs. They do sell better than just publishing one book. However, this is still known as "hope" publishing.

There are a lot more actions to do than just set-and-forget publishing. Passive income doesn't mean you do nothing, it just means you don't have to work anywhere near as hard. You aren't printing your own books and distributing them in the back of your van to local bookstores.

Digital versions means your book can be produced and sold anywhere by anyone on your behalf. You still have to do the marketing and promotion as if your book was traditionally published, just like any business has to do their own promotion.

Book-As-Idea-Containers

What successful authors know (that most beginning authors don't) is that books are idea containers. Those ideas are built into a cohesive whole and don't just have to be ebooks or printed books. Once an idea-container is in digital format, it can be readily converted into other digital forms.

The key reason successful authors do success is because they are publishing in every possible format to every possible outlet. This means you can publish those ideas as:

- ebook
- paperback
- hardback
- audiobook
- audio CD
- video DVD
- course

These seven are the main one's I've found. There are variations, such as Large Print paperbacks and hardbacks, MP3 CD's, and courses in both mini-and-maxi versions. There are also memberships which are built around the data a book series contains. Good fiction books often become movies and wind up as DVD's.

Multiple Eyeballs, Multiple Outlets

Your outlets are many for every single type of book. You can easily name a dozen ebook outlets besides Amazon. Paperbacks and hardbacks are sold globally in local bookstores and chains through perhaps 8-10 main distributors. Audiobooks have around a dozen different places that will sell your books. CD's and DVD's can go to every music store globally (as "spoken word albums") Courses have several places wanting to offer your work, and they can also be built as kits that can be sent out to buyers.

All of these are based on the same basic content you started out with as a document on your computer. They are simply translated into various formats and pushed to the manufacturers or directly to outlets. Printing can be done by POD, which means it will never go out of print. Same with CD's and DVD's. Courses can be delivered online, but also can be set to be created and shipped on demand as well.

The reason this works is that every outlet has their own audience who likes them for one reason or another. No two outlets have exactly the same audience. The general success of these authors is delivering in all possible formats everywhere these readers would be. You want to have your book every way and everywhere.

The digital outlets have unlimited shelf space. While in some cases (like Amazon) this also means your book can be buried alive in their graveyard, it does allow someone who is looking for your specific book to find it. The trick (which we'll get to shortly) is the reader discovering your book and asking for it.

Inflated Egos, Inflated Quality, Deflated Income

The positively *worst* advice you can run into in this area is these guys who always say two things:

> 1. We are slowly losing the stigma of self-publishing our own books.

> 2. To do this, we have to have extremely high quality so that our books look traditionally published.

All that does is tell people to give up on their dreams because it's all just too hard. The two sources I recall offhand pitched their works as "how to" books, but by the end of the book, you see that they didn't follow their own advice. The first turned out to be a celebrity, who could afford to pay a publicist around $20K. The second was a millionaire already, and invested all sorts of other money into his book, while telling people the "cheapest" way to do this. In both cases: narcissist arrogance.

Neither was depending on making a living income from their books. In both cases, having a "book" published just added to the "hey, look at me" approach they had to life already.

The *third worst advice* was from a guy who had never written a book and concluded that no one ever made "real" money from book sales alone. But he was a multi-millionaire and made his money from elsewhere. Again, like the other two, he was talking about something he had no clue about.

(And meanwhile I can name a dozen authors who have worked out how to pull down 6-figures within a couple of years after they buckled down to publishing books that would sell.)

What you are here for, among other reasons, is to learn the hard-boiled nuts-and-bolts about building a decent income from books alone. (And I'm not saying I know all about this. I only write up the research I've had to do to make my own books sell better, and the tests taken.)

One of the basic datums you have to know is that you'll earn your financial freedom by paying your dues. There are no "overnight successes." There are many, many authors who have been writing since there teens or before. Most authors I've followed up (Amanda Hocking, J.K. Rowling, among others) spent at least five years at writing and getting published before they got their first book published that went anywhere. And it was usually the fifth book or more before they started earning any serious income. The only trick is that you didn't see the marketing they had started meanwhile, which usually started before the first book.

I've had my own financial freedom for some years now. It allows research into the points that I know I don't know, to find and test out the ideas people are pitching to see if they work at all.

And you get the benefits from this, as it makes your own research less costly.

For you and I, the better we do this, the more money we make, the more freedom we can experience.

What You Need To Have to Start

1. You have to have your eyes wide open.

2. You have to accept ideas conditionally and test everything you run across - including what you read here.

3. You have to work hard at whatever you do - plan your work, work your plan, revise whenever you need and restart from that point to go forward.

Now, it should also be obvious that the "stigma" is just an archaic idea that no one cares about anymore. It was over when Apple and Amazon set up self-publishing interfaces on their sites. Today, self-published books out-number and out-sell traditionally published books.

The next point isn't so obvious. Inflated quality will have two results:

Great books with poor marketing mostly sell poorly.

Poor books with genius marketing can become "bestsellers."

Both creating great books and getting great marketing are each expensive in terms of both time and money. But there is another way to get your books routinely selling well, whether or not they ever achieve the title of "bestseller":

Decent books with decent marketing can have routinely decent sales.

And enough decent books up there (in a series) can earn you the financial freedom you may be looking for you. As long as they are decently marketed.

To build a decent book that can be decently marketed, we have to go back before the idea was a glimmer in the author's eye...

How to Build a Decent Book

Whoa, no, you don't have to rewrite anything from scratch. We aren't even going to tell you how to publish anything. You know that already (or found someone else who will do it for you.)

Most self-published authors don't start out on the right foot. They pick what they want to write about from their own view, not the reader's. And then they wonder why the book doesn't sell, other than the copy they bought for themselves. (Which was the actual audience for that book - the author. And that is why vanity publishing is called that.)

You have to start out looking through your reader's eyes.

It starts with finding your genre, your niche, your category.

The warning here is that this contradicts all sorts of conventional wisdom. Test everything you get as an idea here. *Especially* what I tell you.

Writing is commercial.

If you want to write for the sake of art, then keep your day job and write your poetry and literary fiction. These don't sell well for various reasons, but they don't sell well. Because you're writing for yourself. If you want to sell books, people have to already want to buy them. People want to buy books they like. To earn your financial freedom through book writing, you have to write and publish decent books that people like and want to buy.

If you only write the single book you've always wanted to write, then you probably only have an audience of one – yourself. (Sure, your friends and family will buy a copy to be supportive, but...)

Writing is <u>commercial</u>.

The better your art (and marketing) the better your book sells.

The breakthrough in this area came via Mark Dawson and his podcast. He was interviewing Adam Croft, who was having a runaway success advertising his latest books to get the earlier ones selling better. But Croft found a fascinating point. All books have a hook. That is the initial idea which sinks into a reader and doesn't let go until they buy the book. Croft found that when he got the right hook, his readers would buy his book. The hook in the ad is the hook of the book.

So Croft started writing the book *after* he wrote the ad copy.

Interestingly, the same research you do to get the hook is what also you do to write the title and description for your Kindle Sales page. And it turned out to make sense because it's all copywriting. Just as the great copywriters will spend hours and days on the headline, it is also just as true for a book. Consider the title to be the headline and description to be body copy for an ad and you'll have it all figured out.

This book started out from research on getting Search Engine Optimization (SEO) right for a Kindle book sales page. Finding the right keywords actually is the research route to writing a commercially viable book.

And the more viable books we publish, the closer we get to financial freedom and the greater we can expand that freedom.

1.2. How This Book Found You Is Why This Book Needed Writing

Unless it was sent you you by email, you probably found this book by searching.

You may not have looked too closely, but here was a book that seemed to have what you were looking for. Answered your questions, promised to solve your problems you've been having.

This book found you by being relevant to your needs and wants.

Most authors don't know how to make their book speak up and talk to the readers that need it. But Amazon prefers to suggest books that talk to their readers effectively.

Effective talking means book sales. And Amazon is all about sales.

Amazon is also known as the "indie authors self-publishing grave yard" because of the traps these authors fall into by not knowing what they need to actually do. Their books just sit there. Most books don't sell. Few sell regularly. A small handful become bestsellers and stay that way.

I had to write this book as this is exactly the scene I fell into. Sure, I was exceptional by publishing enough books in enough areas to start averaging more income than bills. And was able to quit my last day job because of it.

But the marketing of these books was lacking. In fact, I had bought into the false conventional wisdom that just publishing a lot of books was all I needed. Sure, I was able to pay for everything I needed to live a comfortable life, but I was still curious when this much talked-about 6-figure income was going to show up.

Sure, it turned out (as usual) that nothing happens unless and until you make it happen.

So I invested in some courses to find out what else was needed.

The first thing that prompted a face-palm was the fact that my marketing was wrong. There were a ton of thrown-away opportunities with all these published books. In fact, it was surprising that I had gotten any sales at all.

So I then dug in and really learned this area. Because that course just skimmed the surface of what is possible.

Thinking of you and your needs forced me to knuckle down and compile a book about it.

Because we can always use some more successful authors.

Ready to become one of them?

Let's go.

What Keeps Your Books From Selling - They Can't Be Found

2.1. Finding Your Own and Your Books' Relevance

What is relevance?

Relevance is important, as that is what people are looking for. When you look for books in Amazon, you are given what Amazon thinks is most relevant to your request.

Some of these are preformatted, like if you click on "bestsellers" you'll get the top selling books on Amazon, regardless of categories.

But, if you type in "topsellers" in the search bar, you'll get back books that have the word "topseller" or some version of that in their title, subtitle, or descriptions. (Together, these are called "meta-data.")

I don't have access to the algorithms that Amazon uses. What follows in this book is the best guess based on compiling others' best guesses.

- Amazon's search engine apparently first returns the most relevant books based on your search terms.

- If two or more books have the same search terms in their meta-data, then they'll return books in order of sales. But customer experience out-ranks sales (they'll ask you for "fries with that?" in the also-bought section, count on it.)

They push bestsellers, but they also push higher profits. Example: two books have the same keywords in their meta-data, and both sell approximately the same amount of units each day. Amazon will put the $4.99 book higher on the page than the $.99 book.

Now there are a lot of other factors, one of them being your own browsing history and purchases.

Scam Alert

What a lot of shady characters do with Amazon is to put up cheap books and then optimize their meta-data so they are returned highly in Amazon's search results in order to get sales. What is in the book is often nothing to do with what is on the outside.

But these books don't sell for very long. And eventually, when enough customers complain, they are not returned in search results and can even get their author banned. (Of course, the "author" then sets up another account and starts over.)

As a note: you can reverse engineer these scammy books to see what they are targeting as keywords, since often they put them into their descriptions and even embed them in their ebooks. We'll get to this later, but it's an interesting point that came up while testing this research.

The books which continue to sell are well-written and routinely promoted. They don't have to be perfectly written and perfectly promoted. They simply have to be what a person is looking for and fill that need. And they have to be available where a person is looking. That is all there is to marketing and selling a book.

Before we can sell your book, we have to have a book which itself is relevant.

2.2. Making a Relevant Book that Amazon Will Promote

When your book is at the top of the Amazon rankings for any given search, they are being promoted by Amazon.

When a book is selling well, Amazon will even send out emails to buyers recommending that book. This is additional and separate from what we are talking about in this book. But it's a natural follow-up, as Amazon is in the business of making money.

First you have to have a book people are looking for. This is the first step in being relevant.

The trick in sales is to have a book which is in demand, but in small supply. It's not just being "popular." Popular book categories are filled with also-rans and wannabe's. Authors who are following followers and hoping to get a slice of that pie.

You don't want to do "hope" publishing. This is where you write a book and publish it online and then hope it will sell. There is no work to promote is in advance, or run a special sale, or promote it afterwards. It's a set-and-forget mentality. Many of these "hopeful" authors have bought into the false idea that a lot of books alone will get them all to sell better. You do need a lot of books to make a good income, but it's only one of several factors.

What we are discussing in this book is the concept of how to produce a relevant book with relevant meta-data so Amazon will present it where people are looking. This book by itself will help your rankings, but it's part of a wider set of skills you need to have in order to succeed. (See the links at the front and back of this book so you can get related book covering the other skills.)

A Relevant Book Begins Before it is Written

Write that down somewhere, like a post-it note on the edge of your screen.

The old phrase comes to mind: "What begins well, tends to go well."

Your book has to fill pass several tests in order to sell well:

> 1. It has to fill a demand that has inadequate supply.

2. It has to be written well enough to deliver the goods but not be distractive to the reader.

3. It has to be packaged and marketed to be attractive.

The last two points are beyond this book, and we've covered them in broad strokes already. (See other books in this series - link at front and back of this book.)

Let's see how we can find a demand so we can then write a book to fill it.

How to Train Amazon to Recommend Your Book to Buyers

3.1. What Authors Don't Know About Kindle Publishing That Keeps Their Books Unsold

Amazon is known as the self-published author graveyard for good reason. And that reason is *Ignorance*.

The huge demand for self-published books has been met by an overwhelming glut of books that simply don't sell. And that scene created another demand by self-published authors to teach them how to write and publish books that sell. Or, how to get the book they've already written to sell.

But most of these course graduates still don't make their books sell, or even make their money back from those courses or services.

They've missed the boat entirely on several counts.

> 1) They don't realize that Amazon isn't a bookstore, it's a sales-driven search engine.

> 2) They don't understand that a market is based on demand - and they didn't write a book anyone wants to buy.

That first point will help you find and solve the second.

It's all about *relevance*.

There are most commonly three ways people search for your book:

> 1. Directly from someone's link, or by author-title to find a specific book.

> 2. By category to find related books

3. By specific keyword according to their interests.

Now a caveat: no one, except for those who work at Amazon, actually know how the search algorithms work.

From my experience and figuring things out, here's the rough sequence that determines which book comes out on top:

    a. keyword relevance

    b. sales

    c. everything else.

When you do some searches, watch what happens. You'll get books which have no reviews or sales records out-ranking some that have been around for awhile. Because they are more relevant.

In some cases, a new book will out-rank an established book. This can be because Amazon puts new books up front for a given period of time to see how they will sell. (And we'll cover how to use this fact to your own advantage later.)

But the key scenes I've noted is that relevance is first and sales is second. Because Amazon is in the business of selling stuff. They want to give you what you are looking for, and then suggest the bestselling items closest to what you are looking for.

The reviews and backlinks and everything else that can affect a book are alsorans compared to these two. Concentrate on them first and the rest will come along. (Yes, even reviews.)

If you are producing relevant content people are looking for, then you can get sales and reviews and readers and everything else you could want as a successful author. Including money.

But it all starts from the fact that the vast number of authors don't understand how to create and promote relevant content and so they get few or no sales.

It's not all that hard, but we have to cover some basics about how to find your own relevance, so you can create relevant books that people are looking to buy.

3.2. How is Amazon Different From Google?

Simply:

- Amazon returns search results to help you buy.

- Google returns answers to your questions.

More deeply,

- Amazon is paid from selling books (and other things.)

- Google is paid from selling ads.

(Amazon does sell ads, but they haven't proved to be all that effective at this writing.)

Now, all that said, you do want to pay some attention to what Google returns, as you want them to send people looking for an answer to that question to Amazon to buy your book.

And this is where we start into SEO - Search Engine Optimization.

3.3. How to Optimize Your Book for Amazon Kindle and Google

The secret to bestselling books is not just that they are relevant, but that they are optimized to be recommended.

This is known as "Search Engine Optimization." It applies to Amazon (like we covered) as it's a search engine that sells books, not a bookstore.

Of course, we can remind you here that there are scammy ways to apply this material. And that you are not a scammer, so will use this ethically. Again, the scammers have a rough time, as scamming is a J.O.B (just over broke) since they have to constantly be coming out with new scams to replace the old ones which got found out, and have to look over their shoulders constantly to see who has caught onto them and changed the rules.

The best overall discussion about SEO for Amazon that I've found is on Tom Morkes' site (see Appendix). However, he missed the boat in a few areas, which is one reason this book was written.

Another good overview of all things SEO as relates to Amazon Kindle, check out "Amazon Kindle Rankings" from Kindlepreneur (https://kindlepreneur.com/amazon-kindle-rankings-2/)

Most authors start their SEO by having written a decent book that has relevant content for people who are looking for it. Or they can be still doing research to produce it. Either way, we want to know what people are looking for and give it to them where they are looking.

The common words or phrases that people regularly look for are key and are called keywords and keyword phrases. Most of the data you can find on line is about how these are used on Google. And what they say is generally correct - but like all the data you find on writing and publishing (including this book) you need to test everything for yourself to be sure.

A basic to Amazon is to look for "long tail keyword phrases." You want to search the long tail to find your keywords. This is where there are regular sales, but no so much demand that you can't get some of these sales for yourself.

The idea of a long tail was found on Amazon itself. Chris Anderson's research lead to a book, "The Long Tail: Why the Future of Business Is Selling Less of More" (See links in Appendix.) He found that as many book-units were being sold in all these small markets all together as were being sold by the bestseller-units.

3.4. The Two Types of Keywords inside Amazon

Just to be complex, here is some interesting twists that have evolved with Amazon. There are two types of keywords/keyword phrases on Amazon:

1. Category Keywords
2. Search Keywords.

We'll cover finding search keywords separately from this, in an upcoming chapter. What you need to know is that the search keywords go into your book meta-data, and your category keywords are used when you publish via KDP.

When you publish a book, you have a form field that allows you to add up to 7 keywords.

These keywords are actually keyword *phrases* (remember that long tail scene?) And they determine your category. To some degree, they also influence your relevance rankings. When you look up the book on Amazon (or even have a program pull down the book meta-data, as we'll go over soon) you never see these keywords show up again.

My calling these "category" keywords is to remind you that this is how you can get into more categories. As well, those categories are keyword phrases all on their own. In fact, every single word on your book sales page is used to determine relevance. Some words are more popular and that's why they're called "key" words.

There are many categories on Amazon where you can't place your own book. Amazon tells about some of these (see link in Appendix.) But you get into these by putting your book into the (sub) category just above the sub-category you want and then ensuring you put that sub-category name in as a keyword. Meanwhile, you can put in other categories in these keywords and have the very real possibility of getting your book into more than a half-dozen categories. This of course means more ways to possibly get that "bestseller" status for you book.

Frankly, some would say this is wrong. But it's all about the approach you want to take in SEO.

How you find these category keywords we've already covered somewhat, when we found which category we wanted to write the book about. But there's a little more you should know...

How to Author a Book That Amazon Wants to Sell For You

4.1. Finding What Readers What You to Write About

Although this is being bought up now, it's only because you had to understand everything that went before.

Practically, you start with what the audience wants and then write a book for them.

As covered, this isn't what is popular. It's what is wanted that there isn't enough of.

Too often authors have had this backwards (myself included.) They get fascinated by something and then assume the rest of the world is fascinated by it as well. Actually there are almost always *some* people who *might* be fascinated. But are there *enough* to buy whatever it is that they just wrote about? To make a living from book sales? More than likely - not.

This is part of what is called "hope publishing."

Smart authors write what people want to buy. You saw where Adam Croft realized he needed to write starting with the specific hook in a specific genre. "What would you do if you found out you were [enter a dire situation]?"

For non-fiction, it's said to always write the solution to a common unsolved problem. And that can be successful - if not too many have already gotten there first.

So we need to know where there is demand and not enough supply.

You aren't just writing for the money. So you want to find something that is interesting to you and also in demand by buying readers. This is where your passion and the audience's needs overlap. And that is where we'll be able to start creating any amount of income you really want. You deliver what your buying readers think is truly valuable.

With the tools we've already mentioned, Amazon will tell you this.

4.2. Finding Category Keywords - Secret Tools That Work

The trick to making enough income as an author, let alone a nice 6-figure income, is by narrowing down to a profitable niche where people are buying books. These are found in categories.

We want to find our best categories so we write for what people want, and we write what we love, but stay out of categories that have too much competition in them.

Romance is popular, but not in the broad category itself. The best sales are in the subcategories and often the sub-sub categories. Detective novels have probably as many sub-genres (sub-categories.)

You're looking to write and publish in areas that have very low competition, yet there aren't enough books being published, according to the buyers. Profitable income is supplying demand where there is not enough supply. Always has been that way, always will be.

There are some exceptions to any rule, including this one. But you won't know until you research for yourself.

The way Steve Scott and others tell you to find a category is to select a category and look at the sales of the top few and bottom few of the top twenty. The first few should be under 20K in their sales rank. The bottom few should be greater than 50K in sales rank. This means that with a little work, you can wind up on the front page and move up to become a "bestseller" in that category. Meanwhile, people are buying enough of your books to make it profitable.

Dave Chessom of Kindlepreneur has a different (more severe) take:

- It should have fewer than 4 ebooks with an Amazon Best Seller Rank (ABSR) less than of <10,000
- It should have fewer than 7 ebooks with the keyword in their title and or subtitle
- It should have fewer than 2 with Best Seller marks
- At least 2 ebooks should have an ABSR less than 100,000 – shows there are decent sales

The trick to resolving this problem is that there are well over 4,000 categories and subcategories. And they are being added to all the time. (Recently I did a check and found there a couple hundred more have been added over the past two years.)

Of course, you only work on the categories you are interested in, that you have content ideas for. Still, expect to do some slogging work for about a week at this.

Enter BetterBookTools.com Andy Makar built this to take care of a lot of the things that Kindle authors have problems with. Like formatting their descriptions with Kindle-ready HTML and coming up with ideas for books. Mostly, his real value is that when you subscribe to his site (a one-time fee for lifetime access) you can have his program check out programs for you and tell you whether they are viable and are also competitive.

And still, this takes a lot of patience, since the majority of the categories are either making no sales or have too much competition.

So he did it one better. He sets his programs to work and they scrape Amazon to find the profitable categories for you and makes them all available on his website for you - for another one-time fee. Now it only takes minutes to find the best categories. And they are often right besides where you were already looking - or there is a related category which you wouldn't normally think of.

Anyway, check it out for yourself.

So You've Found a Great Category, Now What?

You want to finalize your category keywords. You're going to need about 3-5 categories, actually. Some of them will be next door to the one you have, but can only be gotten into by knowing the keyword you have to put here.

Here's some links that tell you how to do this, and why I call these "category" keywords:

- Kindlepreneur: https://kindlepreneur.com/how-to-unlock-the-secret-kindle-categories/

- Amazon's explanation: https://kdp.amazon.com/help?topicId=A200PDGPEIQX41#keywords

- Lindsay Buroker on how she really leveraged this: http://www.lindsayburoker.com/tips-and-tricks/book-more-categories-amazon-with-keywords/

One handy trick is to scrape that Amazon page with all those hidden category keywords and paste it into a spreadsheet for ready access. This way, you can cross-compare categories where you can get the fastest discovery and sales against alternate categories you can also rank for. One note: just because BBT says a category has a lot of opportunities, it doesn't mean you're going to be able to get into it without these keywords.

In practice, I've found that with seven keywords, you'll still have to narrow down to the ones with the best opportunities.

If *do* you have leftover spaces? Fill this with appropriate keywords for your story genre from different categories. Reason being, even if this doesn't get you additional categories, your book might be relevant for someone simply typing in that category by itself.

What do you do with those leftover category keywords? Make a note of them. When you're ready to craft your description, weave them in as well. Couldn't hurt (as long as you're not just stuffing them.)

Overall, you may want to cross-check the various opportunities this gives you to get the best possible discovery and sales. Some of these categories have some pretty sad sales, but can give you bestseller status and so have your book show up there. With a little work, you should be able to find categories that have both. Again, you can change these later to get into better-selling categories where more people are looking.

- - - -

And now, we get into how to find the most appropriate keywords for search...

4.3. Finding Popular Search Keywords - Another Secret Tool

The old school way to do this was to go through Google's Keyword Planner and find how they ranked these terms. And add anything else they found for you that was getting clicked on.

Then you would take that list and put them into Amazon's search bar to see what Amazon says are actually selling. If that keyword didn't show up in that drop down, you scratched it off your list. Oh, and the only way to get the Amazon keywords was to manually type them by hand.

There are a few tools out there which people have created for this. I like Kindlepreneur's **KDP Rocket** (https://kindlepreneur.com/kdp-rocket-review/) . What this does is to go and get both the Google data and Amazon data for any term you put in. Then you can copy the data on the page and drop it into a spreadsheet. Rinse/repeat.

You'll have the traffic data from Google as well as Amazon, and it won't be colored by what you visited recently.

Once you have your spreadsheet all worked up, then you can sort it to your heart's content and use the best ones which will bring you the most traffic and exposure.

A Cross-Check on Your Kindle Keywords

There is one more tool I use and recommend to update your book's SEO: **Calibre** - this is a free download from https://calibre-ebook.com/ . It's original purpose was to organize your library of books. It's grown from that into a very powerful program. And I'm not going to get into a huge review of how to use this, as it would be a course in itself.

We are going to use it to help find the hottest keywords you should be using.

What it is able to do is to search any book in your library for the available meta-data online. Meaning, it will scrape Amazon for that book. But you don't actually have to own that book in order to scrape that data. Sure, you can go in and select/copy/paste the data off that page. And you'll wind up with a lot of editing to do in order to just get the description.

Calibre has one trick you can use to simply mine the meta-data of the top twenty and let the program do all the heavy lifting.

You set up an "empty" book in Calibre and then enter the full title and author as found on Amazon. Then click to open up the "Edit Metadata" area, which gives you a dialog box. At the bottom of this is a bar which says "download metadata". Calibre will go out and find these books by that title and pull their metadata. Once you OK it to do so, Calibre will enter that data into your library. Repeat this for the rest of the top 20 books in that category.

So you've got your target category. Logically, the books in that category have already been busy describing their book with all the best keywords. (Or so you hope...)

Now, set up 20 empty books,

- enter the titles and authors of the top 20 books in that category,
- have Calibre pull the meta-data in.

Next, copy all that metadata into a single text file (use a plain vanilla text editor for this.)

Go to one of these online keyword extraction sites, such as http://fivefilters.org/term-extraction/ This doesn't guarantee that the most used phrases will be the best keywords, but you will get a list of most common terms and phrases out of your top 20 competitors.

And these will tend to confirm what you've found, and might also give you some additional ideas. Just check any promising ones in KDP Rocket and add them to your spreadsheet if they pan out.

This is Not the Last Word on Keywords

This area is in constant flux. Scammers are constantly finding holes and both Google and Amazon are plugging them as fast as they can. Meanwhile, there are many white hats who simply do this as their hobby to see how high they can get their book ranking on keywords alone.

So do your own searches and test all this data for yourself. Don't just accept what I said. See if it works for you. Only then will you have certainty and the results you want.

Now that we have our keywords, where do we place them?...

4.4. Where to Put Your Search Keywords - Where the Sun Shines.

Search keywords are able to be placed in five places:

1. Title
2. Subtitle
3. Series
4. Description
5. Editorial Reviews

The first four are placed when you put your book up in Kindle through their KDP interface.

And the last one is placed by going into Author Central. (https://authorcentral.amazon.com/) *Note*: when you are there, don't mess with your book description, as you won't be able to change it back without having to email them. The Author Central version is much shorter than the 4000 characters you're given in the KDP interface. Just enter the editorial reviews and exit. If doing that messes up your beautiful description formatting, then contact them.

How and Why You Place These Keywords

Most obviously, they have to make sense the way you use them.

Titles seem to be the exception. These also need to be attractive as a marketing element. They should be catchy. (And if they are going to be extended a series, they need to be trademarked. Don't wait on this like Steve Scott did with "habit stacking" and watch others crowd in on your success. Think "Chicken Soup for the Soul™".)

The fewer words you have in a line of words, the more power they will have to help you rank. Just as it's common for copywriters to spend days on just the title of an article, so there should be some time spent crafting that special title. "Think and Grow Rich" is an excellent example, on many levels.

Subtitles are the work horse in non-fiction, but also can define a fiction work. The trick is to have these words also on the cover. They don't have to be legible on the thumbnail-size views, but Amazon says they need to be there.

Descriptions are seldom read. They are mostly scanned. You want to use bullet-pointed lists, bold, and italic, as well as different-sized headings. This is why you use Amazon-approved simple HTML code to create your description. There are several online editors you can use. I prefer BetterBookTools.com as it gives you a lot more tools as well. Copy your text in there, and then have it do the magic. Then copy the code and put into your submission. It just has to be less thatn 4000 characters total.

You want to use all the characters you can. Because even if readers don't read this material, the Amazon search engine does.

Editorial Reviews are a way to jumpstart your sales conversions. You don't have to wait for people to leave reviews – just enter them here once Amazon approves your book.

Editorial Reviews appear even if the description is mostly hidden. And they show up before the reader reviews. So this is your chance from the outset to get your books converting. Of course, they shouldn't be fake, but I've not seen where Amazon is policing these the way they do reader reviews. Just be sensible, and you should be fine.

4.5. A Cautionary Note About Kindle SEO

The effect of Amazon SEO fades unless refreshed.

Several authors have noted this.

The effects of the keywords you use fade after time. Some note that your category keywords have no effect about three months after you post your book. Others tell that Amazon has an emphasis on new books, and this is what improves the ranks of your earlier ones (also-boughts, related's.)

About every quarter, you should be refreshing your book SEO on Amazon and updating various points. Review your analytics and rankings to see what you might now be better ranking for. So this means a keyword review, using whatever tools you find useful.

You can tweak your cover if you want.

And of course, you can update the content of the ebook itself.

Every update really means a new version of the book, and Amazon will put your "new" book up front for a short while. So regular updating of your meta-data, and revisions of the book itself, will enable your book to be discovered more easily. In short, a solution to the Amazon graveyard scenario.

*The added caution is to change **only** one thing at a time to see if that improves or detracts from rankings or sales. Otherwise, you'll never know what made it go up or down in the rankings.*

You're going to have to program this maintenance into your publishing schedules. Recommended is to have your changes in before the next 90 days pass. (Something to do with their internal promotion algorithms.) While this point is often observed and noted, it is seldom acted on.

4.6 Another SEO Tip Most Self-Publishers Don't Know

Once you've got everything figured out, and you have your series all set up in one sub-sub-sub-genre, you have to know that you're eventually going to be working against yourself. Because you have a single tight set of keywords being used in a single category for a number of books all linked together. Amazon can only show so many also-boughts at any given time.

It's reported that about 10 books in a series will saturate that keyword set. If you're taking my advice and publishing 8 ebooks and 3 collections all over 22 weeks, then you'll "dominate" that search term set on Amazon.

At that point, it's time to re-work your search terms and maybe even genre/category choice to start your next series.

Of course, you can also see how you can keep this up almost indefinitely. We haven't touched on pen names yet (and won't) but there are several good publishing strategies in this area. (Hint.)

Next: How to apply all we've learned to those books you already have published. Maybe we can make them bestsellers again...

Writing A Decent Book (Is Not That Hard)

5.1. Writing Decent Books Based on Research

We mentioned earlier how Adam Croft is writing his book after writing his ad. And also that you get your inspiration from looking over the competition in your category/niche.

What we aren't going to cover here is how to write. The point from the below steps is that when you have your research done, you're set to write your book. (See Appendix if you need more books about writing.)

1. **Find the genre** you can publish the most successful books in. (Betterbooktools.com)

2. **Derive the top keywords** using Kindle Spy and KDP Rocket in conjunction. Sort these on a spreadsheet to get the top terms Amazon gives you.

3. **Use Calibre to pull the meta-data** for the top 20 books in this category.

4. **Work this up as a single text file and extract the benefits.** Read every line of this text to get a feel for what they are saying.

5. **Read the longer reader reviews of each of the top 20** to get what people are saying about these books. Copy/paste any problem areas or benefits into the earlier text file. Also note where the author screwed up in their books and didn't deliver. This action will also tell you more about what buyer persona you are writing for.

6. **From these lists, isolate a common problem area** where people are looking for solutions.

7. **From the problem, distill a crisis and extract the hook you need.**

8. **Write the ad, then plot and write the books.** You can even record the audio as part of your third proof. The main hook will be over-arching, although you'll get a new hook for each book in turn. Best would be to make these a serial so that they have cliff-hangers for the next book to solve.

9. **When you have it proofed, submit it to your "street team"** for their ideas and critique. Fix as necessary.

10. **Repeat 8 and 9 for the next 6 books.** Target yourself for two months to have everything ready. Then launch a new book every two weeks.

The other option is to do this with three short books in order to test the market, then expand into the rest of the series if they do well. You've got six weeks of the first three in that series and two weeks of the collection to test this market. If it takes off, quickly get the next five ready to roll.

5.2. Picking Subjects You Can Write About Forever

Publishing books is a form of content marketing. If you study Joe Pulizzi's works, you'll see quickly how to apply the key material to your own material and make it work and succeed.

One point he covers in his "Content, Inc." is that every person, every company, has a *sweet spot*. That point is the crossing where you are most interested and where your best skill-sets lie. What you are fascinated with, what you could talk about all day, that is the area you'll be able to find endless inspiration. How you produce this most effectively is dependent on what you know how to do best.

And this is why some authors are really performers with a book they published. Another might be a corporate spokesperson with a few books to their credit. And this also explains why some authors write only horror, others only detective stories.

You have to know yourself. Study your own back-trail and see where you've been. Make notes of what excites you and what you'll do instead of the work that sits in front of you. Look over your bookshelves and pick out the ones which you've read several times, the ones with the worn covers, the dog-eared pages. What movies you watch over and over and know a lot of the dialog by heart.

You have to know your sweet spot in order to pick out what to write about.

You have to know your own heart and mind in order to succeed in writing.

As I said, some authors have learned this painfully. Amanda Hocking wrote over 17 complete novels before she had one good enough to publish (and it had errors and typo's.) She had been writing since before she even hit her teens. Herman Melville wrote a lifetime of work. But his greatest achievement, Moby Dick, was a success after he died. You can read about Stephen King's successes and failures in his "On Writing".

The conventional wisdom is that we all can't be as prolific as Shakespeare or Asimov. This is probably not true, like most conventional wisdom. What's probably more true is that those people who use that as an excuse have never figured out what their bliss really is, and have swallowed multiple lies as excuses to simply avoid hard work and accomplish what they are here to do.

Once you know that, and only after you know that, are you ready to start the publishing journey. All that went before that point is just practicing and learning.

The point to all learning is to graduate.

Can You Re-Kindle Book Sales?

6.1. Reviving Earlier Books - Theory

Short of a complete re-write, you can often find a new home for your books that will allow them to sell better.

While Amazon likes new books, they also like books which have been "made to look like new." Books have a pattern of sales that Amazon tracks. This influences where they are placed in searches. If you put a new "face" on your books, then Amazon will offer them the same preferential treatment they give new books.

Like Google and any real book store, they rotate their stock to give readers a look at "new releases." This is a common practice of the traditional book publishers - to put a new cover on an old book and freshen it up.

Now in our case, the change is primarily in our meta-data. And this may require changes to the cover, but often minor ones. If you want to change your subtitle to incorporate new keyword phrases, you'll need those terms on the cover. Changing your title can be done, but is less seldom needed. (As well, this can cause you headaches if you already have a lot of other marketing and landing pages configured for the book's original title.)

6.2. How to Chain Your Books Together So They Recommend the Next

Ideally, your books help sell other books. And this is by recommending them. A very old tactic is to put links to other books in the back of your current one. Often, you'll put an excerpt out of that book. In an ebook, if you do this smart, you'll have your next book ready and can put the live link in there for it.

As Ben Franklin mentioned, hanging together is better than being hanged separately. Getting your books to recommend each other helps sell other books.

Like many of us, we have books out there which just stand alone and so are dying alone. If you revise them with reader magnets front and back, you are doing two things:

> 1) You're telling Amazon that the book has been revised and is "new" again.

> 2) You're setting that book up to link the readers to other books you've also written and getting their email as well.

How to Forge Your Book Chains

You have two reader magnets in the book. The front one should give them a link to a landing page where they receive a special ebook or whitepaper or checklist they can download in exchange for an email. The back one can either also get their email or get a sale. Members-only prices are available for signing up for a free membership (which is contingent on continuing to open emails.)

The reason they are different is that the first one shows up in the Look Inside, and the second can only be gotten by buying the book.

This can go many, many different ways. I'd probably send them to a page where they can get the extra data about this book (videos, notes as images and PDF's, extra lists and so on.) All these options are paid, so they are actually getting an insider's view of things. And on this page, they are also asked to join a membership to get notified of new releases in advance and also access to special options for each book in advance.

But another approach is using that second reader magnet to send them to get the next book in the series. What I would do is to send them to the sales page for that book *on my own site*. That page has the Amazon link (which gives them all the versions there.) It also has a link to Lulu where I give them discounts on the paperbacks, and a third option of Pay-What-You-Want, where they can get a bundle of digital versions of that book.

Sure some would say that you should be sending them directly to Amazon. Well, that link is on the page. But I'm also giving a lot more value to that reader. Also, this tends to interrupt their Amazon addiction.

The point is to use Amazon to build *your* audience and sell *your* books. You don't work for Amazon, you need to put them to work for you.

Then when they get the next book in that series, it's set up the same way.

6.3. And Now What?

Passive income doesn't mean you "put it all on auto-pilot" and "sit back and watch the money roll in."

Passive income still means work, it just means a lot less than having to produce every single thing you sell.

Book marketing has never been "set and forget." You have to regularly run analytics and see what needs tweaking.

If you already have a lot of books out there, you are way ahead of the game. Now you only need to adjust their meta-data to get the best possible amount of sales from them. After that, start running ads to get demand oriented to your own books.

There are limits that any particular set of books will produce. But even the classics continue to sell hundreds of years after their authors death, so you can do a lot better than average if you

- Link them together with reader magnets,

- Build your audience,

- Run ads on Facebook and do other promotions.

Beyond this are other actions you can take in addition to continuing to write and publish. One option is courses, that has been mentioned obliquely. Most successful fiction authors I've followed also now have a non-fiction set of materials they've built into a course. This is offered to affiliate markters who push it to their lists.

The best point is to use the passive income from book publishing to create the lifestyle you want.

Anything is possible at this point.

Life is what you make it, after all.

Over to you. See you on the heights.

Appendix

7.1. Cheat-sheet: How to Write, Market, and Sell Your Library of Decent Books.

Just to get this out in a simple format:

0. Overall, we are

> a. Writing shorter books instead of longer ones so that we can
>
> b. Publish every two weeks and
>
> c. Make more income from the same wordage while also getting Amazon to promote our books.

Everything else about writing engaging books, as well as artful covers and accurate, keyword-targeted meta-data still applies.

I. Getting Started At All

0. Have a goal. Write this down. Review it several times daily. Make this your burning desire.

1. Marketing is started when you decide to get serious about your book sales.

2. At that point, you study successful authors who have mastered marketing, still watching out for those who succumb to "approval fever" and can now make more money giving talks than writing. (Also applies to authors-as-celebrity discovering Affiliate marketing and diversifying into non-fiction courses.)

3. Get a domain name, an email autoresponder service, a web host or hosting service.

4. Create a valuable giveaway that will help people improve their lives. Create a subscription form, landing page, and

thankyou page to deliver this giveaway so people can join your list.

5. Start blogging or podcasting and put the opt-in form prominently on every page (and the home page of your site.)

6. Start doing guest interviews on other podcasts to talk about your upcoming book. (Whatever ideas you have.)

7. Set up the habit of checking your site analytics regularly, as well as sales for any books you've already published.

II Getting Decent Books Made

1. Find the genre you can publish the most successful books in. (Betterbooktools.com)

2. Derive the top keywords using Kindle Spy and KDP Rocket in conjunction. Sort these on a spreadsheet to get the top terms Amazon gives you.

3. Use Calibre to pull the meta-data for the top 20 books in this category.

4. Work this up as a single text file and extract the benefits. Read every line of this text to get a feel for what they are saying.

5. Read the longer reviews of each of the top 20 to get what people are saying about these books. Copy/paste any problem areas or benefits into the earlier text file. Also note where the author screwed up in their books and didn't deliver. This action will also tell you what buyer persona you are writing for.

6. From these lists, isolate a common problem area where people are looking for solutions.

7. From the problem, understand the crisis and extract the hook you need.

8. Plot the book, write the ad, then write the books. Record the audio as part of your third proof. Main hook will be over-arching, although you'll get a new hook for each book in

turn. Best would be to make these a serial so that they have cliff-hangers for the next book to solve.

9. When you have it proofed, submit it to your "street team" for their ideas and critique. Fix as necessary.

10. Repeat 8 and 9 for the next 6 books. You should be able to average a book per week. Target yourself for two months to have everything ready.

III. Beginning the Decent Book Launch

0. You've been continually interviews by podcasters, right? So you've kept their audiences up to speed. Announce an upcoming launch with as many teasers as possible.

00. You've also been emailing your subscribers regularly and keeping them up to speed, as well as pruning off those who never open your emails. Start enlisting their help as the launch is starting.

1. Publish your books two-four weeks apart. Publish them to Amazon and everywhere else. Announce the fact to your list, starting with the street team. Except for the first one, the books are at .99 for about a week and then the price goes up. Second email to full list just before the price goes up.

2. First book is given away to all your readers (as PDF) and published as ebook everywhere possible, using an aggregator such as Lulu, D2D, Smashwords, and priced as Free. Reader Magnet at the back is to get the first collection (first 3 books.) Ask street team for honest reviews. Email all list to let them know when the book was released, and 24 hours before you raise the price.Note: Start checking your sales analytics.

3. Second and third book end up at 2.99 - same reader magnet as the first.

4. First collection is 3.99 and has some additional material in it that aren't in the first three books.

5. Fourth through seventh books are 2.99 - reader magnet is for the second collection.

8. Second collection published at 4.99, also with additional material not in the second set of three books.

9. Mega-collection of all books published at 5.99.

9a. Publish the Createspace version of that mega-collection as a paperback. Also publish the audiobook at the same time. Publish a "spoken word album" through CDBaby. Publish a hardback through Lulu. Get Amazon to link them all up. Time these so that they are available slightly before the ebook collection comes out.

10. Facebook ads can be run mega-collection in order to boost sales for the series as well as other versions. Add FB ads analytics to your regular routines in order to leverage best conversions.

11. Schedule a quarterly review of all your analytics, sales, and actions taken. You'll want to do an update of meta-data on all books, in order of original release, to freshen sales. So schedule this in. Every book needs to be freshened every quarter (3 months) to help Amazon continue to recommend it, so mark your calendar 3 months ahead on each book to do that review and tweaking.

You now have 8 ebooks, 3 collections, 8 thin paperbacks, one regular paperback (can go into libraries, etc.) one hardback, one audiobook, one audio CD set.

IV. Next Decent Book Series

1. Stick to that genre or expand to one next door (a new sub-sub-category, but similar.) Use a different pen name if it's too different from what you've just written about. If a new one, then repeat all the research steps. (This will go faster this time.)

2. Get a hook. Write the ad, Write the book.

3. Repeat the steps above and just continue on with life.

Notes: From your quarterly reviews, you'll see more and more of what you need to streamline to achieve your goals.

You can re-release your earlier books in a series with this plan.

As you get more efficient, you can start releasing your books as they are finalized. You just have to do these steps often enough to be able to keep track of all the moving parts.

In a year's time, you can repeat this four times, giving you a potential of 44 ebooks and their paperbacks, 4 hardbacks, 4 audiobooks, and 4 audio CD's - or 100 properties out there.

Luck to us all.

7.2. About the Author

Dr. Robert C. Worstell has been self-publishing since ebooks were only a gleam in their creator's eye. 2006, to be precise. While operating a working farm, he has published a few hundred books of his own and for other authors. He maintains several active podcasts in addition to several blogs and active websites. His most current work is found at http://LiveSensical.com - and this is where you can contact him.

7.3. Resources

Tools I recommend:

BetterBookTools.com - http://betterbooktools.com/

KDP Rocket - https://kindlepreneur.com/kdp-rocket-review/

Calibre - https://calibre-ebook.com/

LibreOffice - https://www.libreoffice.org/download/

GIMP - https://www.gimp.org/downloads/

Scrivener - https://www.literatureandlatte.com

How to Get Into Hidden Categories

https://kindlepreneur.com/how-to-unlock-the-secret-kindle-categories/

https://kdp.amazon.com/help?topicId=A200PDGPEIQX41

https://jenniferbresnick.com/2013/07/12/the-dirty-little-secret-of-amazon-category-rankings/

http://www.lindsayburoker.com/tips-and-tricks/book-more-categories-amazon-with-keywords/

Amazon SEO Discussion Links

Kindlepreneur/Dave Chessum:

https://kindlepreneur.com/amazon-kindle-rankings-2/

https://kindlepreneur.com/how-to-choose-kindle-keywords/

https://kindlepreneur.com/advanced-google-search-tactics-for-authors/

https://www.semrush.com/blog/amazon-seo-tactics-because-amazon-is-a-search-engine-too/

Tom Morkes

http://tommorkes.com/kindle-seo/

BetterBooksTools - Training

http://www.betterbooktools.com/kindle-best-seller-niche-report-training/

Recommended books:

The Long Tail: Why the Future of Business Is Selling Less of More by Chris Anderson

www.longtail.com/about.html

https://www.amazon.com/dp/B000JMKSE2)

Becoming a Writer by Dorothea Brande

http://amzn.com/B01C6CDI6M

Bibliography

Other books in this series

Visit http://livesensical.com/book-series/publishing-and-writing/

Available on Amazon, Lulu, and as Pay What You Want

Really Simple Writing & Publishing

Learn How to Write, Design, Format, Upload, and Sell Your Own Book for Low Cost or Free.

J'APE: Just Another Publicity Excuse

How to Publish Your (Kindle) Book for Shameless Self-Promotion and Profit

Publish. Profit. Independence.

How to Earn Extra Income and Financial Freedom by Publishing on Your Own

How to Write Less and Profit More

A Rich Adventure in Short Read Kindle Publishing - http://amzn.com/B01AQPPQM0

Writing Serial Fiction in the Real World

A Simple, Tongue-in-Cheek Guide to Writing and Publishing Episodic eBooks for Profit on Amazon (and Elsewhere.)

How to Help Librarians Fall in Love With Your Self-Published Book

...and Get More Sales When They Do.

Cracking the Kindle Sales Code

How to Search Engine Optimize Your Titles and Descriptions so Amazon Promotes Your Book and Recommends Buyers to You at No Cost

An Honest Kindle Booksales Blueprint

How to Break Out of the No-Sales Amazon Self-Publishing Basement and Start Routinely Earning Regular Passive Income From Your Kindle Booksales Without Added Expense or Tricks

- - - - -

A key book to understanding the Amazon Algorithm:

Let's Get Visible: How To Get Noticed And Sell More Books http://amzn.com/B00CPQ6YYI

Odd Links:

NYT: Joys and Hazards of Self-Publishing on the Web by Alan Finder - http://www.nytimes.com/2012/08/16/technology/personaltech/ins-and-outs-of-publishing-your-book-via-the-web.html

Copyright

Disclaimer:

The author and publisher of this Ebook and the accompanying materials have used their best efforts in preparing this Ebook. The author and publisher make no representation or warranties with respect to the accuracy, applicability, fitness, or completeness of the contents of this Ebook. The information contained in this Ebook is strictly for educational purposes. Therefore, if you wish to apply ideas contained in this Ebook, you are taking full responsibility for your actions.

Index

Bonus

Get Related Writing and Publishing Materials From Our Free Library

Instant Access – Join Here

Click or type into your browser:

http://livesensical.com/go/writingbooks/

Preface

The following notes are by no means intended as a rule of thought by which nurses can teach themselves to nurse, still less as a manual to teach nurses to nurse. They are meant simply to give hints for thought to women who have personal charge of the health of others. Every woman, or at least almost every woman, in England has, at one time or another of her life, charge of the personal health of somebody, whether child or invalid, — in other words, every woman is a nurse. Every day sanitary knowledge, or the knowledge of nursing, or in other words, of how to put the constitution in such a state as that it will have no disease, or that it can recover from disease, takes a higher place. It is recognized as the knowledge which everyone ought to have — distinct from medical knowledge, which only a profession can have.

If, then, every woman must, at some time or other of her life, become a nurse, *i.e.*, have charge of somebody's health, how immense and how valuable would be the produce of her united experience if every woman would think how to nurse.

I do not pretend to teach her how, I ask her to teach herself, and for this purpose I venture to give her some hints.

Notes on Nursing: What it is and What it is Not

Disease a reparative process

Shall we begin by taking it as a general principle that all disease, at some period or other of its course, is more or less a reparative process, not necessarily accompanied with suffering: an effort of nature to remedy a process of poisoning or of decay, which has taken place weeks, months, sometimes years beforehand, unnoticed, the termination of the disease being then, while the antecedent process was going on, determined?

If we accept this as a general principle we shall be immediately met with anecdotes and instances to prove the contrary. Just so if we were to take, as a principle — all the climates of the earth are meant to be made habitable for man, by the efforts of man — the objection would be immediately raised, — Will the top of Mont Blanc ever be made habitable? Our answer would be, it will be many thousands of years before we have reached the bottom of Mont Blanc in making the earth healthy. Wait till we have reached the bottom before we discuss the top.

Of the sufferings of disease, disease not always the cause
In watching disease, both in private houses and in public hospitals, the thing which strikes the experienced observer most forcibly is this, that the symptoms or the sufferings generally considered to be inevitable and incident to the disease are very often not symptoms of the disease at all, but of something quite different — of the want of fresh air, or of light, or of warmth, or of quiet, or of cleanliness, or of punctuality and care in the administration of diet, of each or of all of these. And this quite as much in private as in hospital nursing.

The reparative process which Nature has instituted and which we call disease has been hindered by some want of knowledge or attention, in one or in all of these things, and pain, suffering, or interruption of the whole process sets in.

If a patient is cold, if a patient is feverish, if a patient is faint, if he is sick after taking food, if he has a bedsore, it is generally the fault not of the disease, but of the nursing.

What nursing ought to do
I use the word nursing for want of a better. It has been limited to signify little more than the administration of medicines and the application of poultices. It ought to

signify the proper use of fresh air, light, warmth, cleanliness, quiet, and the proper selection and administration of diet — all at the least expense of vital power to the patient.

Nursing the sick little understood

It has been said and written scores of times that every woman makes a good nurse. I believe, on the contrary, that the very elements of nursing are all but unknown.

By this I do not mean that the nurse is always to blame. Bad sanitary, bad architectural, and bad administrative arrangements often make it impossible to nurse. But the art of nursing ought to include such arrangements as alone make what I understand by nursing, possible.

The art of nursing, as now practiced, seems to be expressly constituted to unmake what God had made disease to be, viz., a reparative process.

Nursing ought to assist the reparative process

To recur to the first objection. If we are asked, is such or such a disease a reparative process? Can such an illness be unaccompanied with suffering? Will any care prevent such a patient from suffering this or that? — I humbly say, I do not know. But when you have done away with all that pain and suffering, which in patients are the symptoms not of their disease, but of the absence of one or all of the above-mentioned essentials to the success of Nature's reparative processes, we shall then know what are the symptoms of and the sufferings inseparable from the disease.

Another and the commonest exclamation which will be instantly made is — Would you do nothing, then, in cholera, fever, etc.? — So deep-rooted and universal is the conviction that to give medicine is to be doing something, or rather everything; to give air, warmth, cleanliness, etc., is to do nothing. The reply is that in these and many other similar diseases the exact value of particular remedies and modes of treatment is by no means ascertained, while there is universal experience as to the extreme importance of careful nursing in determining the issue of the disease.

Nursing the well

The very elements of what constitutes good nursing are as little understood for the well as for the sick. The same laws of health or of nursing, for they are in reality the same, obtain among the well as among the sick. The breaking of them produces only a less violent consequence among the former than among the latter, — and this sometimes, not always.

It is constantly objected, — "But how can I obtain this medical knowledge? I am not a doctor. I must leave this to doctors."

Little understood

Oh, mothers of families! You who say this, do you know that one in every seven infants in this civilized land of England perishes before it is one year old? That, in London, two in every five die before they are five years old? And, in the other great cities of England, nearly one out of two[i]? "The life duration of tender babies" (as some Saturn, turned analytical chemist, says) "is the most delicate test" of sanitary conditions. Is all this premature suffering and death necessary? Or did Nature intend mothers to be always accompanied by doctors? Or is it better to learn the piano-forte than to learn the laws which promote the preservation of offspring?

Macaulay somewhere says, that it is extraordinary that, whereas the laws of the motions of the heavenly bodies, far removed as they are from us, are perfectly well understood, the laws of the human mind, which are under our observation all day and every day, are no better understood than they were two thousand years ago.

But how much more extraordinary is it that, whereas what we might call the coxcombries of education — *e.g.*, the elements of astronomy — are now taught to every schoolgirl, neither mothers of families of any class, nor school mistresses of any class, nor nurses of children, nor nurses of hospitals, are taught anything about those laws which God has assigned to the relations of our bodies with the world in which He has put them. In other words, the laws which make these bodies, into which He has put our minds, healthy or unhealthy organs of those minds, are all but unlearnt. Not but that these laws — the laws of life — are in a certain measure understood, but not even mothers think it worth their while to study them — to study how to give their children healthy existences. They call it medical or physiological knowledge, fit only for doctors.

Another objection

We are constantly told, — "But the circumstances which govern our children's health's are beyond our control. What can we do with winds? There is the east wind. Most people can tell before they get up in the morning whether the wind is in the east."

To this one can answer with more certainty than to the former objections. Who is it who knows when the wind is in the east? Not the Highland drover, certainly, exposed to the east wind, but the young lady who is worn out with the want of exposure to fresh air, to sunlight, etc. Put the latter under as good sanitary circumstances as the former, and she too will not know when the wind is in the east.

Table of Contents

I. Ventilation and Warming

First rule of nursing, to keep the air within as pure as the air without

The very first canon of nursing, the first and the last thing upon which a nurse's attention must be fixed, the first essential to the patient, without which all the rest you can do for him is as nothing, with which I had almost said you may leave all the rest alone, is this: <u>To keep the air he breathes as pure as the external air, without chilling him</u>. Yet what is so little attended to? Even where it is thought of at all, the most extraordinary misconceptions reign about it. Even in admitting air into the patient's room or ward, few people ever think, where that air comes from. It may come from a corridor into which other wards are ventilated, from a hall, always unaired, always full of the fumes of gas, dinner, of various kinds of mustiness; from an underground kitchen, sink, washhouse, water-closet, or even, as I myself have had sorrowful experience, from open sewers loaded with filth; and with this the patient's room or ward is aired, as it is called — poisoned, it should rather be said. Always air from the air without, and that, too, through those windows, through which the air comes freshest. From a closed court, especially if the wind do not blow that way, air may come as stagnant as any from a hall or corridor.

Again, a thing I have often seen both in private houses and institutions. A room remains uninhabited; the fire place is carefully fastened up with a board; the windows are never opened; probably the shutters are kept always shut; perhaps some kind of stores are kept in the room; no breath of fresh air can by possibility enter into that room, nor any ray of sun. The air is as stagnant, musty, and corrupt as it can by possibility be made. It is quite ripe to breed small-pox, scarlet fever, diphtheria, or anything else you please[ii].

Yet the nursery, ward, or sick room adjoining will positively be aired by having the door opened into that room. Or children will be put into that room, without previous preparation, to sleep.

A short time ago a man walked into a back-kitchen in Queen square, and cut the throat of a poor consumptive creature, sitting by the fire. The murderer did not deny the act, but simply said, "It's all right." Of course he was mad.

But in our case, the extraordinary thing is that the victim says, "It's all right," and that we are not mad. Yet, although we "nose" the murderers, in the musty unaired un-sunned room, the scarlet fever which is behind the door, or the fever and hospital gangrene which are stalking among the crowded beds of a hospital ward, we say, "It's all right."

Without chill

With a proper supply of windows, and a proper supply of fuel in open fire places, fresh air is comparatively easy to secure when your patient or patients are in bed. Never be afraid of open windows then. People don't catch cold in bed. This is a popular fallacy. With proper bedclothes and hot bottles, if necessary, you can always keep a patient warm in bed, and well ventilate him at the same time.

But a careless nurse, be her rank and education what it may, will stop up every cranny and keep a hot-house heat when her patient is in bed, — and, if he is able to get up, leave him comparatively unprotected. The time when people take cold (and there are many ways of taking cold, besides a cold in the nose,) is when they first get up after the two-fold exhaustion of dressing and of having had the skin relaxed by many hours, perhaps days, in bed, and thereby rendered more incapable of re-action. Then the same temperature which refreshes the patient in bed may destroy the patient just risen. And common sense will point out that, while purity of air is essential, a temperature must be secured which shall not chill the patient. Otherwise the best that can be expected will be a feverish re-action.

To have the air within as pure as the air without, it is not necessary, as often appears to be thought, to make it as cold.

In the afternoon again, without care, the patient whose vital powers have then risen often finds the room as close and oppressive as he found it cold in the morning. Yet the nurse will be terrified, if a window is opened[iii].

Open windows

I know an intelligent humane house surgeon who makes a practice of keeping the ward windows open. The physicians and surgeons invariably close them while going their rounds; and the house surgeon very properly as invariably opens them whenever the doctors have turned their backs.

In a little book on nursing, published a short time ago, we are told, that "with proper care it is very seldom that the windows cannot be opened for a few minutes twice in the day to admit fresh air from without." I should think not; nor twice in the hour either. It only shows how little the subject has been considered.

What kind of warmth desirable

Of all methods of keeping patients warm the very worst certainly is to depend for heat on the breath and bodies of the sick. I have known a medical officer keep his ward windows hermetically closed, thus exposing the sick to all the dangers of an infected atmosphere, because he was afraid that, by admitting fresh air, the temperature of the ward would be too much lowered. This is a destructive fallacy.

To attempt to keep a ward warm at the expense of making the sick repeatedly breathe their own hot, humid, putrescent atmosphere is a certain way to delay recovery or to destroy life.

Bedrooms almost universally foul

Do you ever go into the bedrooms of any persons of any class, whether they contain one, two, or twenty people, whether they hold sick or well, at night, or before the windows are opened in the morning, and ever find the air anything but unwholesomely close and foul? And why should it be so? And of how much importance it is that it should not be so? During sleep, the human body, even when in health, is far more injured by the influence of foul air than when awake. Why can't you keep the air all night, then, as pure as the air without in the rooms you sleep in? But for this, you must have sufficient outlet for the impure air you make yourselves to go out; sufficient inlet for the pure air from without to come in. You must have open chimneys, open windows, or ventilators; no close curtains round your beds; no shutters or curtains to your windows, none of the contrivances by which you undermine your own health or destroy the chances of recovery of your sick[iv].

When warmth must be most carefully looked to

A careful nurse will keep a constant watch over her sick, especially weak, protracted, and collapsed cases, to guard against the effects of the loss of vital heat by the patient himself. In certain diseased states much less heat is produced than in health; and there is a constant tendency to the decline and ultimate extinction of the vital powers by the call made upon them to sustain the heat of the body. Cases where this occurs should be watched with the greatest care from hour to hour, I had almost said from minute to minute. The feet and legs should be examined by the hand from time to time, and whenever a tendency to chilling is discovered, hot bottles, hot bricks, or warm flannels, with some warm drink, should be made use of until the temperature is restored. The fire should be, if necessary, replenished. Patients are frequently lost in the latter stages of disease from want of attention to such simple precautions. The nurse may be trusting to the patient's diet, or to his medicine, or to the occasional dose of stimulant which she is directed to give him, while the patient is all the while sinking from want of a little external warmth. Such cases happen at all times, even during the height of summer. This fatal chill is most apt to occur towards early morning at the period of the lowest temperature of the twenty-four hours, and at the time when the effect of the preceding day's diets is exhausted.

Generally speaking, you may expect that weak patients will suffer cold much more in the morning than in the evening. The vital powers are much lower. If they are feverish at night, with burning hands and feet, they are almost sure to be chilly and shivering in the morning. But nurses are very fond of heating the foot-warmer at night, and of neglecting it in the morning, when they are busy. I should reverse the matter.

All these things require common sense and care. Yet perhaps in no one single thing is so little common sense shown, in all ranks, as in nursing[v].

Cold air not ventilation, nor fresh air a method of chill

The extraordinary confusion between cold and ventilation, in the minds of even well educated people, illustrates this. To make a room cold is by no means necessarily to ventilate it. Nor is it at all necessary, in order to ventilate a room, to chill it. Yet, if a nurse finds a room close, she will let out the fire, thereby making it closer, or she will open the door into a cold room, without a fire, or an open window in it, by way of improving the ventilation. The safest atmosphere of all for a patient is a good fire and an open window, excepting in extremes of temperature. (Yet no nurse can ever be made to understand this.) To ventilate a small room without draughts of course requires more care than to ventilate a large one.

Night air

Another extraordinary fallacy is the fear of night air. What air can we breathe at night but night air? The choice is between pure night air from without and foul night air from within. Most people prefer the latter. An unaccountable choice. What will they say if it is proved to be true that fully one-half of all the disease we suffer from is occasioned by people sleeping with their windows shut? An open window most nights in the year can never hurt anyone. This is not to say that light is not necessary for recovery. In great cities, night air is often the best and purest air to be had in the twenty-four hours. I could better understand in towns shutting the windows during the day than during the night, for the sake of the sick. The absence of smoke, the quiet, all tend to making night the best time for airing the patients. One of our highest medical authorities on Consumption and Climate has told me that the air in London is never as good as after ten o'clock at night.

Air from the outside: Open your windows, shut your doors

Always air your room, then, from the outside air, if possible. Windows are made to open; doors are made to shut — a truth which seems extremely difficult of apprehension. I have seen a careful nurse airing her patient's room through the door, near to which were two gaslights, (each of which consumes as much air as eleven men), a kitchen, a corridor, the composition of the atmosphere in which consisted of gas, paint, foul air, never changed, full of effluvia[1], including a current of sewer air from an ill-placed sink, ascending in a continual stream by a well-staircase, and discharging themselves constantly into the patient's room. The window of the said room, if opened, was all that was desirable to air it. Every room must be aired from without — every passage from without. But the fewer passages there are in a hospital the better.

Smoke

If we are to preserve the air within as pure as the air without, it is needless to say that the chimney must not smoke. Almost all smoky chimneys can be cured — from the bottom, not from the top. Often it is only necessary to have an inlet for air to supply the fire, which is feeding itself, for want of this, from its own chimney. On the other hand, almost all chimneys can be made to smoke by a careless nurse, who lets the fire get low and then overwhelms it with coal; not, as we verily believe, in order to spare herself trouble, (for very rare is unkindness to the sick), but from not thinking what she is about.

Airing damp things in a patient's room

In laying down the principle that the first object of the nurse must be to keep the air breathed by her patient as pure as the air without, it must not be forgotten that everything in the room which can give off effluvia, besides the patient, evaporates itself into his air. And it follows that there ought to be nothing in the room, excepting him, which can give off effluvia or moisture. Out of all damp towels, etc., which becomes dry in the room, the damp, of course, goes into the patient's air. Yet this "of course" seems as little thought of, as if it

---

[1] An unpleasant or harmful odor, secretion, or discharge.

were an obsolete fiction. How very seldom you see a nurse who acknowledges by her practice that nothing at all ought to be aired in the patient's room, that nothing at all ought to be cooked at the patient's fire! Indeed the arrangements often make this rule impossible to observe.

If the nurse be a very careful one, she will, when the patient leaves his bed, but not his room, open the sheets wide, and throw the bed clothes back, in order to air his bed. And she will spread the wet towels or flannels carefully out upon a horse, in order to dry them. Now either these bedclothes and towels are not dried and aired, or they dry and air themselves into the patient's air. And whether the damp and effluvia do him most harm in his air or in his bed, I leave to you to determine, for I cannot.

Effluvia from excreta

Even in health people cannot repeatedly breathe air in which they live with impunity, on account of its becoming charged with unwholesome matter from the lungs and skin. In disease where everything given off from the body is highly noxious and dangerous, not only must there be plenty of ventilation to carry off the effluvia, but everything which the patient passes must be instantly removed away, as being more noxious than even the emanations from the sick.

Of the fatal effects of the effluvia from the excreta it would seem unnecessary to speak, were they not so constantly neglected. Concealing the utensils behind the valance to the bed seems all the precaution which is thought necessary for safety in private nursing. Did you but think for one moment of the atmosphere under that bed, the saturation of the underside of the mattress with the warm evaporations, you would be startled and frightened too!

Chamber utensils without lids

The use of any chamber utensil *without a lid*[vi] should be utterly abolished, whether among sick or well. You can easily convince yourself of the necessity of this absolute rule, by taking one with a lid, and examining the underside of that lid. It will be found always covered, whenever the utensil is not empty, by condensed offensive moisture. Where does that go, when there is no lid?

Earthenware, or if there is any wood, highly polished and varnished wood, are the only materials fit for patients' utensils. The very lid of the old abominable close-stool is enough to breed a pestilence. It becomes saturated with offensive matter, which scouring is only wanted to bring out. I prefer an earthenware lid as being always cleaner. But there are various good new-fashioned arrangements.

Abolish slop pails

A slop pail[2] should never be brought into a sick room. It should be a rule invariable, rather more important in the private house than elsewhere, that the utensil should be carried directly to the water-closet, emptied there, rinsed there, and brought back. There should always be water and a cock in every water-closet for rinsing. But even if there is not, you must carry water there to rinse with. I have actually seen, in the private sick room, the utensils emptied into the foot-pan, and put back un-rinsed under the bed. I can hardly say which is most abominable, whether to do this or to rinse the utensil *in* the sick room. In the best hospitals it is now a rule that no slop-pail shall ever be brought into the wards, but that the utensils shall be carried direct to be emptied and rinsed

---

[2] A large pail used to receive waste water from a washbasin or chamber pot.

at the proper place. I would it were so in the private house.

Fumigations

Let no one ever depend upon fumigations, "disinfectants," and the like, for purifying the air. The offensive thing, not its smell, must be removed. A celebrated medical lecturer began one day "Fumigations, gentlemen, are of essential importance. They make such an abominable smell that they compel you to open the window." I wish all the disinfecting fluids invented made such an "abominable smell" that they forced you to admit fresh air. That would be a useful invention.

II. Health of Houses

There are five essential points in securing the health of houses[vii]:

1. Pure air.
2. Pure water.
3. Efficient drainage.
4. Cleanliness.
5. Light.

Without these, no house can be healthy. And it will be unhealthy just in proportion as they are deficient.

Pure air

To have pure air, your house must be so constructed as that the outer atmosphere shall find its way with ease to every corner of it. House architects hardly ever consider this. The object in building a house is to obtain the largest interest for the money, not to save doctors' bills to the tenants. But, if tenants should ever become as wise as to refuse to occupy unhealthily constructed houses, and if Insurance Companies should ever come to understand their interest so thoroughly as to pay a Sanitary Surveyor to look after the houses where their clients live, speculative architects would speedily be brought to their senses. As it is, they build what pays best. And there are always people foolish enough to take the houses they build. And if in the course of time the families die off, as is so often the case, nobody ever thinks of blaming any but Providence[viii] for the result. Ill-informed medical men aid in sustaining the delusion, by laying the blame on "current contagions." Badly constructed houses do for the healthy what badly constructed hospitals do for the sick. Once insure that the air in a house is stagnant, and sickness is certain to follow.

Pure water

Pure water is more generally introduced into houses than it used to be, thanks to the exertions of the sanitary reformers. Within the last few years, a large part of London was in the daily habit of using water polluted by the drainage of its sewers and water closets. This has happily been remedied. But, in many parts of the country, well water of a very impure kind is used for domestic purposes. And when epidemic disease shows itself, persons using such water are almost sure to suffer.

Drainage

It would be curious to ascertain by inspection, how many houses in London are really well drained. Many people would say, surely all or most of them. But many people have no idea in what good drainage consists. They think that a sewer in the street and a pipe leading to it from the house is good drainage. All the while the sewer may be nothing but a laboratory from which epidemic disease and ill health is being distilled into the house. No house with any untrapped drain pipe communicating immediately with a sewer, whether it is from water closet, sink, or gully-grate, can ever be healthy. An untrapped sink may at any time spread fever or septicemia[3] among the inmates of a palace.

Sinks

The ordinary oblong sink is an abomination. That great surface of stone, which is always left wet, is always exhaling into the air. I have known whole houses and hospitals smell of the sink. I have met just as strong a stream of sewer air coming up the back staircase of a grand London house from the sink, as I have ever met at Scutari; and I have seen the rooms in that house all ventilated by the open doors, and the passages all

---

[3] Blood poisoning, esp. that caused by bacteria or their toxins.

unventilated by the closed windows, in order that as much of the sewer air as possible might be conducted into and retained in the bedrooms. It is wonderful.

Another great evil in house construction is carrying drains underneath the house. Such drains are never safe. All house drains should begin and end outside the walls. Many people will readily admit, as a theory, the importance of these things. But how few are there who can intelligently trace disease in their households to such causes! Is it not a fact, that when scarlet fever, measles, or smallpox appears among the children, the very first thought which occurs is, "where" the children can have "caught" the disease? And the parents immediately run over in their minds all the families with whom they may have been. They never think of looking at home for the source of the mischief. If a neighbor's child is seized with smallpox, the first question which occurs is whether it had been vaccinated. No one would undervalue vaccination; but it becomes of doubtful benefit to society when it leads people to look abroad for the source of evils which exist at home.

Cleanliness

Without cleanliness, within and without your house, ventilation is comparatively useless. In certain foul districts of London, poor people used to object to open their windows and doors because of the foul smells that came in. Rich people like to have their stables and dunghill near their houses. But does it ever occur to them that with many arrangements of this kind it would be safer to keep the windows shut than open? You cannot have the air of the house pure with dung heaps under the windows. These are common all over London. And yet people are surprised that their children, brought up in large "well-aired" nurseries and bedrooms suffer from children's epidemics. If they studied Nature's laws in the matter of children's health, they would not be so surprised.

There are other ways of having filth inside a house besides having dirt in heaps. Old papered walls of years' standing, dirty carpets, unclean furniture, are just as ready sources of impurity to the air as if there were a dung-heap in the basement. People are so unaccustomed from education and habits to consider how to make a home healthy, that they either never think of it at all, and take every disease as a matter of course, to be "resigned to" when it comes "as from the hand of Providence;" or if they ever entertain the idea of preserving the health of their household as a duty, they are very apt to commit all kinds of "negligence's and ignorance's" in performing it.

Light

A dark house is always an unhealthy house, always an ill-aired house, always a dirty house. Want of light stops growth, and promotes scrofula, rickets, etc., among the children.

People lose their health in a dark house, and if they get ill they cannot get well again in it. More will be said about this farther on.

Three common errors in managing the health of houses

Three out of many "negligence's and ignorance's" in managing the health of houses generally, I will here mention as specimens

1. That the female head in charge of any building does not think it necessary to visit every hole and corner of it every day. How can she expect those who are under her to be more careful to maintain her house in a healthy condition than she who is in charge of it?

2. That it is not considered essential to air, to sun, and to clean rooms while uninhabited; which is simply

ignoring the first elementary notion of sanitary
things, and laying the ground ready for all kinds of
diseases.

3. That the window, and one window, is considered
    enough to air a room. Have you never observed that
    any room without a fireplace is always close?

And, if you have a fireplace, would you cram it up not
only with a chimney-board, but perhaps with a great
wisp of brown paper, in the throat of the chimney — to
prevent the soot from coming down, you say? If your
chimney is foul, sweep it; but don't expect that you can
ever air a room with only one aperture; don't suppose
that to shut up a room is the way to keep it clean. It is
the best way to foul the room and all that is in it. Don't
imagine that if you, who are in charge, don't look to all
these things yourself, those under you will be more
careful than you are. It appears as if the part of a
mistress now is to complain of her servants and to
accept their excuses — not to show them how there
need be neither complaints made nor excuses.

Head in charge must see to House Hygiene, not do it herself

But again, to look to all these things yourself does not
mean to do them yourself. "I always open the
windows," the head in charge often says. If you do it, it
is by so much the better, certainly, than if it were not
done at all. But can you not insure that it is done when
not done by yourself? Can you insure that it is not
undone when your back is turned? This is what being
"in charge" means. And a very important meaning it is,
too. The former only implies that just what you can do
with your own hands is done. The latter that what ought
to be done is always done.

Does God think of these things so seriously?

And now, you think these things trifles, or at least exaggerated. But what you "think" or what I "think" matters little. Let us see what God thinks of them. God always justifies His ways. While we are thinking, He has been teaching. I have known cases of hospital septicemia quite as severe in handsome private houses as in any of the worst hospitals, and from the same cause, viz., foul air. Yet nobody learnt the lesson. Nobody learnt *anything* at all from it. They went on *thinking* — thinking that the sufferer had scratched his thumb, or that it was singular that "all the servants" had "whitlows," or that something was "much about this year; there is always sickness in our house." This is a favorite mode of thought — leading *not* to inquire what is the uniform cause of these general "whitlows," but to stifle all inquiry. In what sense is "sickness" being "always there," a justification of its being "there" at all?

How does He carry out His laws?

I will tell you what was the cause of this hospital septicemia being in that large private house. It was that the sewer air from an ill-placed sink was carefully conducted into all the rooms by sedulously opening all the doors; and closing all the passage windows. It was that the slops were emptied into the foot pans; — it was that the utensils were never properly rinsed; — it was that the chamber crockery was rinsed with dirty water; — it was that the beds were never properly shaken, aired, picked to pieces, or changed. It was that the carpets and curtains were always musty; — it was that the furniture was always dusty; it was that the papered walls were saturated with dirt; — it was that the floors were never cleaned; — it was that the uninhabited rooms were never sunned, or cleaned, or aired; — it was that the cupboards were always reservoirs of foul air; — it was that the windows were always tight shut up at night; — it was that no window was ever systematically opened, even in the day, or that the right window was not opened. A person gasping for air might open a window for himself. But the servants were not taught to open the windows, to shut the doors; or they opened the windows upon a dank well between high walls, not upon the airier court; or they opened the room doors into the unaired halls and passages, by way of airing the rooms. Now all this is not fancy, but fact. How does He teach His laws? In that handsome house I have known in one summer three cases of hospital septicemia, one of phlebitis, two of consumptive cough: all the immediate products of foul air. When, in temperate climates, a house is unhealthier in summer than in winter, it is a certain sign of something wrong. Yet nobody learns the lesson. Yes, God always justifies His ways. He is teaching while you are not learning. This poor body loses his finger, that one loses his life. And all from the most easily preventable causes[ix].

Physical degeneration in families; Its causes

The houses of the grandmothers and great grandmothers of this generation, at least the country houses, with front door and back door always standing open, winter and summer, and a thorough draught always blowing through — with all the scrubbing, and cleaning, and polishing, and scouring which used to go on, the grandmothers, and still more the great grandmothers, always out of doors and never with a bonnet on except to go to church, these things entirely account for the fact so often seen of a great grandmother, who was a tower of physical vigor descending into a grandmother perhaps a little less vigorous but still sound as a bell and healthy to the core, into a mother languid and confined to her carriage and house, and lastly into a daughter sickly and confined to her bed. For, remember, even with a general decrease of mortality you may often find a race thus degenerating and still oftener a family. You may see poor little feeble washed-out rags, children of a noble stock, suffering morally and physically, throughout their useless, degenerate lives, and yet people who are going to marry and to bring more such into the world, will consult nothing but their own convenience as to where they are to live, or how they are to live.

Don't make your sickroom into a ventilating shaft for the whole house

With regard to the health of houses where there is a sick person, it often happens that the sick room is made a ventilating shaft for the rest of the house. For while the house is kept as close, unaired, and dirty as usual, the window of the sick room is kept a little open always and the door occasionally. Now, there are certain sacrifices which a house with one sick person in it does make to that sick person: it ties up its knocker; it lays straw before it in the street. Why can't it keep itself thoroughly clean and unusually well aired, in deference to the sick person?

Infection

We must not forget what, in ordinary language, is called "Infection[x];" — a thing of which people are generally so afraid that they frequently follow the very practice in regard to it which they ought to avoid. Nothing used to be considered so infectious or contagious as small pox; and people not very long ago used to cover up patients with heavy bed clothes, while they kept up large fires and shut the windows. Small pox, of course, under this régime, is very "infectious." People are somewhat wiser now in their management of this disease. They have ventured to cover the patients lightly and to keep the windows open; and we hear much less of the "infection" of small pox than we used to do. But do people in our days act with more wisdom on the subject of "infection" in fevers — scarlet fever, measles, etc. — than their forefathers did with small pox? Does not the popular idea of "infection" involve that people should take greater care of themselves than of the patient? that, for instance, it is safer not to be too much with the patient, not to attend too much to his wants? Perhaps the best illustration of the utter absurdity of this view of duty in attending on "infectious" diseases is afforded by what was very recently the practice, if it is not so even now, in some of the European lazarets[4] — in which the plague-patient used to be condemned to the horrors of filth, overcrowding, and want of ventilation, while the medical attendant was ordered to examine the patient's tongue through an opera-glass and to toss him a lancet to open his abscesses with!

True nursing ignores infection, except to prevent it. Cleanliness and fresh air from open windows, with unremitting attention to the patient, are the only defence a true nurse either asks or needs.

Wise and humane management of the patient is the best safeguard against infection.

Why must children have measles, etc.?

There are not a few popular opinions, in regard to which it is useful at times to ask a question or two. For example, it is commonly thought that children must have what are commonly called "children's epidemics," "current contagions," etc., in other words, that they are born to have measles, whooping cough, perhaps even scarlet fever, just as they are born to cut their teeth, if they live.

Now, do tell us, why must a child have measles?

---

[4] A hospital treating contagious diseases.

Oh because, you say, we cannot keep it from infection — other children have measles — and it must take them — and it is safer that it should.

But why must other children have measles? And if they have, why must yours have them too?

If you believed in and observed the laws for preserving the health of houses which inculcate cleanliness, ventilation, white-washing, and other means, and which, by the way, are laws, as implicitly as you believe in the popular opinion, for it is nothing more than an opinion, that your child must have children's epidemics, don't you think that upon the whole your child would be more likely to escape altogether?

III. Petty Management

All the results of good nursing, as detailed in these notes, may be spoiled or utterly negative by one defect, viz.: in petty management, or, in other words, by not knowing how to manage that what you do when you are there, shall be done when you are not there. The most devoted friend or nurse cannot be always there. Nor is it desirable that she should. And she may give up her health, all her other duties, and yet, for want of a little management, be not one-half so efficient as another who is not one-half so devoted, but who has this art of multiplying herself — that is to say, the patient of the first will not really be so well cared for, as the patient of the second.

It is as impossible in a book to teach a person in charge of sick how to manage, as it is to teach her how to nurse. Circumstances must vary with each different case. But it is possible to press upon her to think for herself: Now what does happen during my absence? I am obliged to be away on Tuesday. But fresh air or punctuality is not less important to my patient on Tuesday than it was on Monday. Or: At 10 p.m. I am never with my patient; but quiet is of no less consequence to him at 10 than it was at 5 minutes to 10.

Curious as it may seem, this very obvious consideration occurs comparatively to few, or, if it does occur, it is only to cause the devoted friend or nurse to be absent fewer hours or fewer minutes from her patient — not to arrange so as that no minute and no hour shall be for her patient without the essentials of her nursing.

Illustrations of the want of it

A very few instances will be sufficient, not as precepts, but as illustrations.

Strangers coming into the sick room

A strange washerwoman, coming late at night for the "things," will burst in by mistake to the patient's sickroom, after he has fallen into his first doze, giving him a shock, the effects of which are irremediable, though he himself laughs at the cause, and probably never even mentions it. The nurse who is, and is quite right to be, at her supper, has not provided that the washerwoman shall not lose her way and go into the wrong room.

Sickroom airing the whole house

The patient's room may always have the window open. But the passage outside the patient's room, though provided with several large windows, may never have one open. Because it is not understood that the charge of the sickroom extends to the charge of the passage. And thus, as often happens, the nurse makes it her business to turn the patient's room into a ventilating shaft for the foul air of the whole house.

Uninhabited room fouling the whole house

An uninhabited room, a newly painted room[xi], an unclean closet or cupboard, may often become a reservoir of foul air for the whole house, because the person in charge never thinks of arranging that these places shall be always aired, always cleaned; she merely opens the window herself "when she goes in."

Delivery and non-delivery of letters and messages

An agitating letter or message may be delivered, or an important letter or message not delivered; a visitor whom it was of consequence to see, may be refused, or one whom it was of still more consequence not to see may be admitted — because the person in charge has never asked herself this question, What is done when I am not there?[xii]

At all events, one may safely say, a nurse cannot be with the patient, open the door, eat her meals, take a message, all at one and the same time. Nevertheless the person in charge never seems to look the impossibility in the face.

Add to this that the attempting this impossibility does more to increase the poor Patient's hurry and nervousness than anything else.

Partial measures such as "being always in the way" yourself, increase instead of saving the patient's anxiety. Because they must be only partial.

It is never thought that the patient remembers these things if you do not. He has not only to think whether the visit or letter may arrive, but whether you will be in the way at the particular day and hour when it may arrive. So that your partial measures for "being in the way" yourself, only increase the necessity for his thought. Whereas, if you could but arrange that the thing should always be done whether you are there or not, he need never think at all about it.

For the above reasons, whatever a patient can do for himself, it is better, i.e. less anxiety, for him to do for himself, unless the person in charge has the spirit of management.

It is evidently much less exertion for a patient to answer a letter for himself by return of post, than to have four conversations, wait five days, have six anxieties before it is off his mind, before the person who is to answer it has done so.

Apprehension, uncertainty, waiting, expectation, fear of surprise, do a patient more harm than any exertion. Remember, he is face to face with his enemy all the time, internally wrestling with him, having long imaginary conversations with him. You are thinking of something else. "Rid him of his adversary quickly," is a first rule with the sick.[xiii]

For the same reasons, always tell a patient and tell him beforehand when you are going out and when you will be back, whether it is for a day, an hour, or ten minutes. You fancy perhaps that it is better for him if he does not find out your going at all, better for him if you do not make yourself "of too much importance" to him; or else you cannot bear to give him the pain or the anxiety of the temporary separation.

No such thing. You ought to go, we will suppose. Health or duty requires it. Then say so to the patient openly. If you go without his knowing it, and he finds it out, he never will feel secure again that the things which depend upon you will be done when you are away, and in nine cases out of ten he will be right. If you go out without telling him when you will be back, he can take no measures nor precautions as to the things which concern you both, or which you do for him.

What is the cause of half the accidents which happen?

If you look into the reports of trials or accidents, and especially of suicides, or into the medical history of fatal cases, it is almost incredible how often the whole thing turns upon something which has happened because "he," or still oftener "she," "was not there." But it is still more incredible how often, how almost always this is accepted as a sufficient reason, a justification; why, the very fact of the thing having happened is the proof of its not being a justification. The person in charge was quite right not to be "there", he was called away for quite sufficient reason, or he was away for a daily recurring and unavoidable cause: yet no provision was made to supply his absence. The fault was not in his "being away," but in there being no management to supplement his "being away." When the sun is under a total eclipse or during his nightly absence, we light candles. But it would seem as if it did not occur to us that we must also supplement the person in charge of sick or of children, whether under an occasional eclipse or during a regular absence.

In institutions where many lives would be lost and the effect of such want of management would be terrible and patent, there is less of it than in the private house.[xiv]

But in both, let whoever is in charge keep this simple question in her head (not, how can I always do this right thing myself, but) how can I provide for this right thing to be always done?

Then, when anything wrong has actually happened in consequence of her absence, which absence we will supposed to have been quite right, let her question still be (not, how can I provide against any more of such absences? which is neither possible nor desirable, but) how can I provide against anything wrong arising out of my absence?

What it is to be "in charge"

How few men, or even women, understand, either in great or in little things, what it is the being "in charge" — I mean, know how to carry out a "charge." From the most colossal calamities, down to the most trifling accidents, results are often traced (or rather not traced) to such want of someone "in charge" or of his knowing how to be "in charge." A short time ago the bursting of a funnel-casing on board the finest and strongest ship that ever was built, on her trial trip, destroyed several lives and put several hundred in jeopardy — not from any undetected flaw in her new and untried works — but from a tap being closed which ought not to have been closed — from what every child knows would make its mother's teakettle burst. And this simply because no one seemed to know what it is to be "in charge," or who was in charge. Nay more, the jury at the inquest actually altogether ignored the same, and apparently considered the tap "in charge," for they gave as a verdict "accidental death."

This is the meaning of the word, on a large scale. On a much smaller scale, it happened, a short time ago, that an insane person burnt herself slowly and intentionally to death, while in her doctor's charge and almost in her nurse's presence. Yet neither was considered "at all to blame." The very fact of the accident happening proves its own case. There is nothing more to be said. Either they did not know their business or they did not know how to perform it.

To be "in charge" is certainly not only to carry out the proper measures yourself but to see that everyone else does so too; to see that no one either willfully or ignorantly thwarts or prevents such measures. It is neither to do everything yourself nor to appoint a number of people to each duty, but to ensure that each does that duty to which he is appointed. This is the meaning which must be attached to the word by (above all) those "in charge" of sick, whether of numbers or of individuals, (and indeed I think it is with individual sick that it is least understood. One sick person is often waited on by four with less precision, and is really less cared for than ten who are waited on by one; or at least than 40 who are waited on by 4; and all for want of this one person "in charge.)"

It is often said that there are few good servants now: I say there are few good mistresses now. As the jury seems to have thought the tap was in charge of the ship's safety, so mistresses now seem to think the house is in charge of itself. They neither know how to give orders, nor how to teach their servants to obey orders — i.e. to obey intelligently, which is the real meaning of all discipline.

Again, people who are in charge often seem to have a pride in feeling that they will be "missed," that no one can understand or carry on their arrangements, their system, books, accounts, etc., but themselves. It seems to me that the pride is rather in carrying on a system, in keeping stores, closets, books, accounts, etc., so that anybody can understand and carry them on—so that, in case of absence or illness, one can deliver everything up to others and know that all will go on as usual, and that one shall never be missed.

Why hired nurses give so much trouble

Note: — It is often complained, that professional nurses, brought into private families, in case of sickness, make themselves intolerable by "ordering about" the other servants, under plea of not neglecting the patient. Both things are true; the patient is often neglected, and the servants are often unfairly "put upon." But the fault is generally in the want of management of the head in charge. It is surely for her to arrange both that the nurse's place is, when necessary, supplemented, and that the patient is never neglected — things with a little management quite compatible, and indeed only attainable together. It is certainly not for the nurse to "order about" the servants.

IV. Noise

Unnecessary noise

Unnecessary noise, or noise that creates an expectation in the mind, is that which hurts a patient. It is rarely the loudness of the noise, the effect upon the organ of the ear itself, which appears to affect the sick. How well a patient will generally bear, *e.g.*, the putting up of a scaffolding close to the house, when he cannot bear the talking, still less the whispering, especially if it be of a familiar voice, outside his door.

There are certain patients, no doubt, especially where there is slight concussion or other disturbance of the brain, who are affected by mere noise. But intermittent noise, or sudden and sharp noise, in these as in all other cases, affects far more than continuous noise — noise with jar far more than noise without. Of one thing you may be certain, that anything which wakes a patient suddenly out of his sleep will invariably put him into a state of greater excitement, do him more serious, aye, and lasting mischief, than any continuous noise, however loud.

Never let a patient be waked out of his first sleep

Never to allow a patient to be waked, intentionally or accidentally, is a *sine qua non*[5] of all good nursing. If he is roused out of his first sleep, he is almost certain to have no more sleep. It is a curious but quite intelligible fact that, if a patient is waked after a few hours' instead of a few minutes' sleep, he is much more likely to sleep again. Because of pain, like irritability of brain, perpetuates and intensifies itself. If you have gained a respite of either in sleep you have gained more than the mere respite. Both the probability of recurrence and of the same intensity will be diminished; whereas both will

---

[5] An essential condition; a thing that is absolutely necessary.

be terribly increased by want of sleep. This is the reason
why sleep is so all important. This is the reason why a
patient waked in the early part of his sleep loses not
only his sleep, but his power to sleep. A healthy person
who allows himself to sleep during the day will lose his
sleep at night. But it is exactly the reverse with the sick
generally; the more they sleep the better will they be
able to sleep.

Noise which excites expectation

I have often been surprised at the thoughtlessness,
(resulting in cruelty, quite unintentionally) of friends or
of doctors who will hold a long conversation just in the
room or passage adjoining to the room of the patient,
who is either every moment expecting them to come in,
or who has just seen them, and knows they are talking
about him. If he is an amiable patient, he will try to
occupy his attention elsewhere and not to listen — and
this makes matters worse — for the strain upon his
attention and the effort he makes are so great that it is
well if he is not worse for hours after. Whispered
conversation in the room if it is a whispered
conversation in the same room, then it is absolutely
cruel; for it is impossible that the patient's attention
should not be involuntarily strained to hear. Walking on
tip-toe, doing anything in the room very slowly, are
injurious, for exactly the same reasons. A firm light
quick step, a steady quick hand are the desiderata[6]; not
the slow, lingering, shuffling foot, the timid, uncertain
touch. Slowness is not gentleness, though it is often
mistaken for such; quickness, lightness, and gentleness
are quite compatible. Again, if friends and doctors did
but watch, as nurses can and should watch, the features
sharpening, the eyes growing almost wild, of fever
patients who are listening for the entrance from the

---

[6] Something that is needed or wanted.

corridor of the persons whose voices they are hearing there, these would never run the risk again of creating such expectation, or irritation of mind. — Such unnecessary noise has undoubtedly induced or aggravated delirium in many cases. I have known such — in one case death ensued. It is but fair to say that this death was attributed to fright. It was the result of a long whispered conversation, within sight of the patient, about an impending operation; but anyone who has known the more than stoicism, the cheerful coolness, with which the certainty of an operation will be accepted by any patient, capable of bearing an operation at all, if it is properly communicated to him, will hesitate to believe that it was mere fear which produced, as was averred, the fatal result in this instance. It was rather the uncertainty, the strained expectation as to what was to be decided upon.

Or just outside the door

I need hardly say that the other common cause, namely, for a doctor or friend to leave the patient and communicate his opinion on the result of his visit to the friends just outside the patient's door, or in the adjoining room, after the visit, but within hearing or knowledge of the patient is, if possible, worst of all.

Noise of female dress

It is, I think, alarming, peculiarly at this time, when the female inkbottles are perpetually impressing upon us "woman's" "particular worth and general missionaries'," to see that the dress of women is daily more and more unfitting them for any "mission," or usefulness at all. It is equally unfitted for all poetic and all domestic purposes. A man is now a handier and far less objectionable being in a sickroom than a woman. Compelled by her dress, every woman now either shuffles or waddles — only a man can cross the floor of a sickroom without shaking it! What is become of woman's light step? — the firm, light, quick step we have been asking for?

Unnecessary noise, then, is the most cruel absence of care which can be inflicted either on sick or well. For, in all these remarks, the sick are only mentioned as suffering in a greater proportion than the well from precisely the same causes.

Unnecessary (although slight) noise injures a sick person much more than necessary noise (of a much greater amount).

Patient's repulsion to nurses who rustle

All doctrines about mysterious affinities and aversions will be found to resolve themselves very much, if not entirely, into presence or absence of care in these things.

A nurse who rustles (I am speaking of nurses professional and unprofessional) is the horror of a patient, though perhaps he does not know why.

The fidget of silk and of crinoline, the rattling of keys, the creaking of stays and of shoes, will do a patient more harm than all the medicines in the world will do him good.

The noiseless steps of woman, the noiseless drapery of woman, are mere figures of speech in this day. Her skirts (and well if they do not throw down some piece of furniture) will at least brush against every article in the room as she moves.[xv]

Again, one nurse cannot open the door without making everything rattle. Or she opens the door unnecessarily often, for want of remembering all the articles that might be brought in at once.

A good nurse will always make sure that no door or window in her patient's room shall rattle or creak; that no blind or curtain shall, by any change of wind through the open window, be made to flap — especially will she be careful of all this before she leaves her patients for the night. If you wait till your patients tell you, or remind you of these things, where is the use of their having a nurse? There are more shy than exacting patients, in all classes; and many a patient passes a bad night, time after time, rather than remind his nurse every night of all the things she has forgotten.

If there are blinds to your windows, always take care to have them well up, when they are not being used. A little piece slipping down, and flapping with every draught, will distract a patient.

Hurry peculiarly hurtful to sick

All hurry or bustle is peculiarly painful to the sick. And when a patient has compulsory occupations to engage him, instead of having simply to amuse himself, it becomes doubly injurious. The friend who remains standing and fidgeting about while a patient is talking business to him, or the friend who sits and proses, the one from an idea of not letting the patient talk, the other from an idea of amusing him, — each is equally inconsiderate. Always sit down when a sick person is talking business to you, show no signs of hurry, give complete attention and full consideration if your advice is wanted, and go away the moment the subject is ended.

How to visit the sick and not hurt them

Always sit within the patient's view, so that when you speak to him he has not painfully to turn his head round in order to look at you. Everybody involuntarily looks at the person speaking. If you make this act a wearisome one on the part of the patient you are doing him harm. So also if by continuing to stand you make him continuously raise his eyes to see you. Be as motionless as possible, and never gesticulate in speaking to the sick.

Never make a patient repeat a message or request, especially if it be some time after. Occupied patients are often accused of doing too much of their own business. They are instinctively right. How often you hear the person, charged with the request of giving the message or writing the letter, say half an hour afterwards to the patient, "Did you appoint 12 o'clock?" or, "What did you say was the address?" or ask perhaps some much more agitating question — thus causing the patient the effort of memory, or worse still, of decision, all over again. It is really less exertion to him to write his letters himself. This is the almost universal experience of occupied invalids.

This brings us to another caution. Never speak to an invalid from behind, nor from the door, nor from any distance from him, nor when he is doing anything.

The official politeness of servants in these things is so grateful to invalids, that many prefer, without knowing why, having none but servants about them.

These things not fancy

These things are not fancy. If we consider that, with sick as with well, every thought decomposes some nervous matter, — that decomposition as well as re-composition of nervous matter is always going on, and more quickly with the sick than with the well, — that, to obtrude abruptly another thought upon the brain while it is in the act of destroying nervous matter by thinking, is calling upon it to make a new exertion, — if we consider these things, which are facts, not fancies, we shall remember that we are doing positive injury by interrupting, by "startling a fanciful" person, as it is called. Alas! it is no fancy.

Interruption damaging to sick

If the invalid is forced, by his avocations, to continue occupations requiring much thinking, the injury is doubly great. In feeding a patient suffering under delirium or stupor you may suffocate him, by giving him his food suddenly, but if you rub his lips gently with a spoon and thus attract his attention, he will swallow the food unconsciously, but with perfect safety. Thus it is with the brain. If you offer it a thought, especially one requiring a decision, abruptly, you do it a real not fanciful injury. Never speak to a sick person suddenly; but, at the same time, do not keep his expectation on the tiptoe.

And to well

This rule, indeed, applies to the well quite as much as to the sick. I have never known persons who exposed themselves for years to constant interruption who did not muddle away their intellects by it at last. The process with them may be accomplished without pain. With the sick, pain gives warning of the injury.

Keeping a patient standing

Do not meet or overtake a patient who is moving about in order to speak to him, or to give him any message or letter. You might just as well give him a box on the ear. I have seen a patient fall flat on the ground who was standing when his nurse came into the room. This was an accident which might have happened to the most careful nurse. But the other is done with intention. A patient in such a state is not going to the East Indies. If you would wait ten seconds, or walk ten yards further, any promenade he could make would be over. You do not know the effort it is to a patient to remain standing for even a quarter of a minute to listen to you. If I had not seen the thing done by the kindest nurses and friends, I should have thought this caution quite superfluous.[xvi]

Patients dread surprise

Patients are often accused of being able to "do much more when nobody is by." It is quite true that they can. Unless nurses can be brought to attend to considerations of the kind of which we have given here but a few specimens, a very weak patient finds it really much less exertion to do things for himself than to ask for them. And he will, in order to do them, (very innocently and from instinct) calculate the time his nurse is likely to be absent, from a fear of her "coming in upon" him or speaking to him, just at the moment when he finds it quite as much as he can do to crawl from his bed to his chair, or from one room to another, or down stairs, or out of doors for a few minutes. Some extra call made upon his attention at that moment will quite upset him. In these cases you may be sure that a patient in the state we have described does not make such exertions more than once or twice a day, and probably much about the same hour every day. And it is hard, indeed, if nurse and friends cannot calculate so as to let him make them undisturbed. Remember, that many patients can walk who cannot stand or even sit up. Standing is, of all positions, the most trying to a weak patient.

Everything you do in a patient's room, after he is "put up" for the night, increases tenfold the risk of his having a bad night. But, if you rouse him up after he has fallen asleep, you do not risk, you secure him a bad night.

One hint I would give to all who attend or visit the sick, to all who have to pronounce an opinion upon sickness or its progress. Come back and look at your patient *after* he has had an hour's animated conversation with you. It is the best test of his real state we know. But never pronounce upon him from merely seeing what he does, or how he looks, during such a conversation. Learn also carefully and exactly, if you can, how he passed the night after it.

Effects of over-exertion on sick

People rarely, if ever, faint while making an exertion. It is after it is over. Indeed, almost every effect of over-exertion appears after, not during such exertion. It is the highest folly to judge of the sick, as is so often done, when you see them merely during a period of excitement. People have very often died of that which, it has been proclaimed at the time, has "done them no harm[xvii]."

Remember never to lean against, sit upon, or unnecessarily shake, or even touch the bed in which a patient lies. This is invariably a painful annoyance. If you shake the chair on which he sits, he has a point by which to steady himself, in his feet. But on a bed or sofa, he is entirely at your mercy, and he feels every jar you give him all through him.

Difference between real and fancy patients

In all that we have said, both here and elsewhere, let it be distinctly understood that we are not speaking of hypochondriacs. To distinguish between real and fancied disease forms an important branch of the education of a nurse. To manage fancy patients forms an important branch of her duties. But the nursing which real and that which fancied patients require is of different, or rather of opposite, character. And the latter will not be spoken of here. Indeed, many of the symptoms which are here mentioned are those which distinguish real from fancied disease.

It is true that hypochondriacs very often do that behind a nurse's back which they would not do before her face. Many such I have had as patients who scarcely ate anything at their regular meals; but if you concealed food for them in a drawer, they would take it at night or in secret. But this is from quite a different motive. They do it from the wish to conceal. Whereas the real patient will often boast to his nurse or doctor, if these do not shake their heads at him, of how much he has done, or eaten, or walked. To return to real disease.

Conciseness necessary with Sick

Conciseness and decision are, above all things, necessary with the sick. Let your thought expressed to them be concisely and decidedly expressed. What doubt and hesitation there may be in your own mind must never be communicated to theirs, not even (I would rather say especially not) in little things. Let your doubt be to yourself, your decision to them. People who think outside their heads, the whole process of whose thought appears, like Homer's, in the act of secretion, who tell everything that led them towards this conclusion and away from that, ought never to be with the sick.

Irresolution most painful to them

Irresolution is what all patients most dread. Rather than meet this in others, they will collect all their data, and make up their minds for themselves. A change of mind in others, whether it is regarding an operation, or re-writing a letter, always injures the patient more than the being called upon to make up his mind to the most dreaded or difficult decision. Farther than this, in very many cases, the imagination in disease is far more active and vivid than it is in health. If you propose to the patient change of air to one place one hour, and to another the next, he has, in each case, immediately constituted himself in imagination the tenant of the place, gone over the whole premises in idea, and you have tired him as much by displacing his imagination, as if you had actually carried him over both places.

Above all leave the sick room quickly and come into it quickly, not suddenly, not with a rush. But don't let the patient be wearily waiting for when you will be out of the room or when you will be in it. Conciseness and decision in your movements, as well as your words, are necessary in the sick room, as necessary as absence of hurry and bustle. To possess yourself entirely will ensure you from either failing — either loitering or hurrying.

What a patient must not have to see to

If a patient has to see, not only to his own but also to his nurse's punctuality, or perseverance, or readiness, or calmness, to any or all of these things, he is far better without that nurse than with her — however valuable and handy her services may otherwise be to him, and however incapable he may be of rendering them to himself.

Reading aloud

With regard to reading aloud in the sick room, my experience is that when the sick are too ill to read to themselves, they can seldom bear to be read to. children, eye patients, and uneducated persons are exceptions, or where there is any mechanical difficulty in reading. People who like to be read to, have generally not much the matter with them; while in fevers, or where there is much irritability of brain, the effort of listening to reading aloud has often brought on delirium. I speak with great diffidence; because there is an almost universal impression that it is *sparing* the sick to read aloud to them. But two things are certain:

Read aloud slowly, distinctly, and steadily to the sick

(1.) If there is some matter which *must* be read to a sick person, do it slowly. People often think that the way to get it over with least fatigue to him is to get it over in least time. They gabble; they plunge and gallop through the reading. There never was a greater mistake. Houdin, the conjuror, says that the way to make a story seem short is to tell it slowly. So it is with reading to the sick. I have often heard a patient say to such a mistaken reader, "Don't read it to me; tell it me."[xviii] Unconsciously he is aware that this will regulate the plunging, the reading with unequal paces, slurring over one part, instead of leaving it out altogether, if it is unimportant, and mumbling another. If the reader lets his own attention wander, and then stops to read up to himself, or finds he has read the wrong bit, then it is all over with the poor patient's chance of not suffering. Very few people know how to read to the sick; very few read aloud as pleasantly even as they speak. In reading they sing, they hesitate, they stammer, they hurry, they mumble; when in speaking they do none of these things. Reading aloud to the sick ought always to be rather slow, and exceedingly distinct, but not mouthing — rather monotonous, but not sing song — rather loud, but not noisy — and, above all, not too long. Be very sure of what your patient can bear. Ever read aloud by fits and starts to the sick.

(2.) The extraordinary habit of reading to oneself in a sick room, and reading aloud to the patient any bits which will amuse him or more often the reader, is unaccountably thoughtless. What *do* you think the patient is thinking of during your gaps of non-reading? Do you think that he amuses himself upon what you have read for precisely the time it pleases you to go on reading to yourself, and that his attention is ready for something else at precisely the time it pleases you to begin reading again? Whether the person thus read to be sick or well, whether he be doing nothing or doing something else while being thus read to, the self-absorption and want of observation of the person, who does it, is equally difficult to understand — although very often the read*ee* is too amiable to say how much it disturbs him.

People overhead

One thing more: — From the flimsy manner in which most modern houses are built, where every step on the stairs, and along the floors, is felt all over the house; the higher the story, the greater the vibration. It is inconceivable how much the sick suffer by having anybody overhead. In the solidly built old houses, which, fortunately, most hospitals are, the noise and shaking is comparatively trifling. But it is a serious cause of suffering, in lightly built houses, and with the irritability peculiar to some diseases. Better far put such patients at the top of the house, even with the additional fatigue of stairs, if you cannot secure the room above them being untenanted; you may otherwise bring on a state of restlessness which no opium will subdue. Do not neglect the warning, when a patient tells you that he "Feels every step above him to cross his heart." Remember that every noise a patient cannot *see* partakes of the character of suddenness to him; and I am persuaded that patients with these peculiarly irritable nerves are positively less injured by having persons in the same room with them than overhead, or separated by only a thin compartment. Any sacrifice to secure silence for these cases is worthwhile, because no air, however good, no attendance, however careful, will do anything for such cases without quiet.

Music

Note: — The effect of music upon the sick has been scarcely at all noticed. In fact, its expensiveness, as it is now, makes any general application of it quite out of the question. I will only remark here, that wind instruments, including the human voice, and stringed instruments, capable of continuous sound, have generally a beneficent effect — while the piano-forte, with such instruments as have *no* continuity of sound, has just the reverse. The finest piano-forte playing will damage the sick, while an air, like "Home, sweet home," or "Assisa a piè d'un salice," on the most ordinary grinding organ will sensibly soothe them — and this quite independent of association.

V. Variety

Variety a means of recovery

To any but an old nurse, or an old patient, the degree would be quite inconceivable to which the nerves of the sick suffer from seeing the same walls, the same ceiling, the same surroundings during a long confinement to one or two rooms.

The superior cheerfulness of persons suffering severe paroxysms of pain over that of persons suffering from nervous debility has often been remarked upon, and attributed to the enjoyment of the former of their intervals of respite. I incline to think that the majority of cheerful cases are to be found among those patients who are not confined to one room, whatever their suffering, and that the majority of depressed cases will be seen among those subjected to a long monotony of objects about them.

The nervous frame really suffers as much from this as the digestive organs from long monotony of diet, as *e.g.* the soldier from his twenty-one years' "boiled beef."

Color and form means of recovery

The effect in sickness of beautiful objects, of variety of objects, and especially of brilliancy of color is hardly at all appreciated.

Such cravings are usually called the "fancies" of patients. And often doubtless patients have "fancies," as, e.g. when they desire two contradictions. But much more often, their (so called) "fancies" are the most valuable indications of what is necessary for their recovery. And it would be well if nurses would watch these (so called) "fancies" closely.

I have seen, in fevers (and felt, when I was a fever patient myself) the most acute suffering produced from the patient (in a hut) not being able to see out of window, and the knots in the wood being the only view.

I shall never forget the rapture of fever patients over a bunch of bright colored flowers. I remember (in my own case) a nosegay of wild flowers being sent me, and from that moment recovery becoming more rapid.

This is no fancy.

People say the effect is only on the mind. It is no such thing. The effect is on the body, too. Little as we know about the way in which we are affected by form, by color, and light, we do know this, that they have an actual physical effect.

Variety of form and brilliancy of color in the objects presented to patients are actual means of recovery.

But it must be *slow* variety, *e.g.*, if you show a patient ten or twelve engravings successively, ten-to-one that he does not become cold and faint, or feverish, or even sick; but hang one up opposite him, one on each successive day, or week, or month, and he will revel in the variety.

Flowers

The folly and ignorance which reign too often supreme over the sickroom cannot be better exemplified than by this. While the nurse will leave the patient stewing in a corrupting atmosphere, the best ingredient of which is carbonic acid; she will deny him, on the plea of unhealthiness, a glass of cut-flowers, or a growing plant. Now, no one ever saw "overcrowding" by plants in a room or ward. And the carbonic acid they give off at nights would not poison a fly. Nay, in overcrowded rooms, they actually absorb carbonic acid and give off oxygen. Cut flowers also decompose water and produce oxygen gas. It is true there are certain flowers, *e.g.*, lilies, the smell of which is said to depress the nervous system. These are easily known by the smell, and can be avoided.

Effect of body on mind

Volumes are now written and spoken upon the effect of the mind upon the body. Much of it is true. But I wish a little more was thought of the effect of the body on the mind. You who believe yourselves overwhelmed with anxieties, but are able every day to walk up Regent-street, or out in the country, to take your meals with others in other rooms, etc., etc., you little know how much your anxieties are thereby lightened; you little know how intensified they become to those who can have no change[xix]; how the very walls of their sick rooms seem hung with their cares; how the ghosts of their troubles haunt their beds; how impossible it is for them to escape from a pursuing thought without some help from variety.

A patient can just as much move his leg when it is fractured as change his thoughts when no external help from variety is given him. This is, indeed, one of the main sufferings of sickness; just as the fixed posture is one of the main sufferings of the broken limb.

Help the sick to vary their thoughts

It is an ever recurring wonder to see educated people, who call themselves nurses, acting thus. They vary their own objects, their own employments many times a day; and while nursing (!) some bed-ridden sufferer, they let him lie there staring at a dead wall, without any change of object to enable him to vary his thoughts; and it never even occurs to them, at least to move his bed so that he can look out of window. No, the bed is to be always left in the darkest, dullest, remotest, part of the room[xx].

I think it is a very common error among the well to think that "with a little more self-control" the sick might, if they choose, "dismiss painful thoughts" which "aggravate their disease," etc. Believe me, almost *any* sick person, who behaves decently well, exercises more self-control every moment of his day than you will ever know till you are sick yourself. Almost every step that crosses his room is painful to him; almost every thought that crosses his brain is painful to him; and if he can speak without being savage, and look without being unpleasant, he is exercising self-control.

Suppose you have been up all night, and instead of being allowed to have your cup of tea, you were to be told that you ought to "exercise self-control," what should you say? Now, the nerves of the sick are always in the state that yours are in after you have been up all night.

Supply to the sick the defect of manual labor

We will suppose the diet of the sick to be cared for. Then, this state of nerves is most frequently to be relieved by care in affording them a pleasant view, a judicious variety as to flowers,[xxi] and pretty things. Light by itself will often relieve it. The craving for "the return of day," which the sick so constantly evince, is generally nothing but the desire for light, the remembrance of the relief which a variety of objects before the eye affords to the harassed sick mind.

Again, every man and every woman has some amount of manual employment, excepting a few fine ladies, who do not even dress themselves, and who are virtually in the same category, as to nerves, as the sick. Now, you can have no idea of the relief which manual labor is to you — of the degree to which the deprivation of manual employment increases the peculiar irritability from which many sick suffer.

A little needlework, a little writing, a little cleaning, would be the greatest relief the sick could have, if they could do it; these *are* the greatest relief to you, though you do not know it. Reading, though it is often the only thing the sick can do, is not this relief. Bearing this in mind, bearing in mind that you have all these varieties of employment which the sick cannot have, bear also in mind to obtain for them all the varieties which they can enjoy.

I need hardly say that I am well aware that excess in needlework, in writing, in any other continuous employment, will produce the same irritability that defect in manual employment (as one cause) produces in the sick.

VI. Taking Food

Want of attention to hours of taking food

Every careful observer of the sick will agree in this that thousands of patients are annually starved in the midst of plenty, from want of attention to the ways which alone make it possible for them to take food. This want of attention is as remarkable in those who urge upon the sick to do what is quite impossible to them, as in the sick themselves who will not make the effort to do what is perfectly possible to them.

For instance, to the large majority of very weak patients it is quite impossible to take any solid food before 11 A.M., nor then, if their strength is still further exhausted by fasting till that hour. For weak patients have generally feverish nights and, in the morning, dry mouths; and, if they could eat with those dry mouths, it would be the worse for them. A spoonful of beef-tea, of arrowroot and wine, of egg flip, every hour, will give them the requisite nourishment, and prevent them from being too much exhausted to take at a later hour the solid food, which is necessary for their recovery. And every patient who can swallow at all can swallow these liquid things, if he chooses. But how often do we hear a mutton chop, an egg, a bit of bacon, ordered to a patient for breakfast, to whom (as a moment's consideration would show us) it must be quite impossible to masticate such things at that hour.

Again, a nurse is ordered to give a patient a teacup full of some article of food every three hours. The patient's stomach rejects it. If so, try a tablespoon full every hour: if this will not do, a teaspoon full every quarter of an hour.

I am bound to say, that I think more patients are lost by want of care and ingenuity in these momentous minutes in private nursing than in public hospitals. And I think there is more of the *entente cordiale*[7] to assist one another's hands between the doctor and his head nurse in the latter institutions, than between the doctor and the patient's friends in the private house.

Life often hangs upon minutes in taking food

If we did but know the consequences which may ensue, in very weak patients, from ten minutes' fasting or repletion, (I call it repletion when they are obliged to let too small an interval elapse between taking food and some other exertion, owing to the nurse's unpunctuality), we should be more careful never to let this occur. In very weak patients there is often a nervous difficulty of swallowing, which is so much increased by any other call upon their strength that, unless they have their food punctually at the minute, which minute again must be arranged so as to fall in with no other minute's occupation, they can take nothing till the next respite occurs — so that an unpunctuality or delay of ten minutes may very well turn out to be one of two or three hours. And why is it not as easy to be punctual to a minute? Life often literally hangs upon these minutes.

In acute cases, where life or death is to be determined in a few hours, these matters are very generally attended to, especially in hospitals; and the number of cases is large where the patient is, as it were, brought back to life by exceeding care on the part of the doctor or nurse, or both, in ordering and giving nourishment with minute selection and punctuality.

Patients often starved to death in chronic cases

But, in chronic cases, lasting over months and years, where the fatal issue is often determined at last by mere protracted starvation, I had rather not enumerate the instances which I have known where a little ingenuity,

---

1.   [7] A friendly understanding.

and a great deal of perseverance, might, in all probability, have averted the result. The consulting the hours when the patient can take food, the observation of the times, often varying, when he is most faint, the altering seasons of taking food, in order to anticipate and prevent such times — all this, which requires observation, ingenuity, and perseverance (and these really constitute the good nurse), might save more lives than we wot of.

Food never to be left by the patient's side
To leave the patient's untested food by his side, from meal to meal, in hopes that he will eat it in the interval, is simply to prevent him from taking any food at all. I have known patients literally incapacitated from taking one article of food after another, by this piece of ignorance. Let the food come at the right time, and be taken away, eaten or uneaten, at the right time; but never let a patient have "something always standing" by him, if you don't wish to disgust him of everything.

On the other hand, I have known a patient's life saved (he was sinking for want of food) by the simple question, put to him by the doctor, "But is there no hour when you feel you could eat?" "Oh, yes," he said, "I could always take something at — o'clock and — o'clock." The thing was tried and succeeded. Patients very seldom, however, can tell this; it is for you to watch and find it out.

Patient had better not see more food than his own
A patient should, if possible, not see or smell either the food of others, or a greater amount of food than he himself can consume at one time, or even hear food talked about or see it in the raw state. I know of no exception to the above rule. The breaking of it always induces a greater or less incapacity of taking food.

In hospital wards it is of course impossible to observe all this; and in single wards, where a patient must be continuously and closely watched, it is frequently impossible to relieve the attendant, so that his or her own meals can be taken out of the ward. But it is not the less true that, in such cases, even where the patient is not himself aware of it, his possibility of taking food is limited by seeing the attendant eating meals under his observation. In some cases the sick are aware of it, and complain. A case where the patient was supposed to be insensible, but complained as soon as able to speak, is now present to my recollection.

Remember, however, that the extreme punctuality in well-ordered hospitals, the rule that nothing shall be done in the ward while the patients are having their meals, go far to counterbalance what unavoidable evil there is in having patients together. I have often seen the private nurse go on dusting or fidgeting about in a sick room all the while the patient is eating, or trying to eat.

That the more alone an invalid can be when taking food, the better, is unquestionable; and, even if he must be fed, the nurse should not allow him to talk, or talk to him, especially about food, while eating.

When a person is compelled, by the pressure of occupation, to continue his business while sick, it ought to be a rule Without Any Exception Whatever, that no one shall bring business to him or talk to him while he is taking food, nor go on talking to him on interesting subjects up to the last moment before his meals, nor make an engagement with him immediately after, so that there be any hurry of mind while taking them.

Upon the observance of these rules, especially the first, often depends the patient's capability of taking food at all, or, if he is amiable and forces himself to take food, of deriving any nourishment from it.

You cannot be too careful as to quality in sick diet

A nurse should never put before a patient milk that is
sour, meat or soup that is turned, an egg that is bad, or
vegetables underdone. Yet often I have seen these
things brought in to the sick in a state perfectly
perceptible to every nose or eye except the nurse's. It is
here that the clever nurse appears; she will not bring in
the peccant[8] article, but, not to disappoint the patient,
she will whip up something else in a few minutes.
Remember that sick cookery should half do the work of
your poor patient's weak digestion. But if you further
impair it with your bad articles, I know not what is to
become of him or of it.

If the nurse is an intelligent being, and not a mere
carrier of diets to and from the patient, let her exercise
her intelligence in these things. How often we have
known a patient eat nothing at all in the day, because
one meal was left un-tasted (at that time he was
incapable of eating), at another the milk was sour, the
third was spoiled by some other accident. And it never
occurred to the nurse to extemporize some expedient, —
it never occurred to her that as he had had no solid food
that day, he might eat a bit of toast (say) with his tea in
the evening, or he might have some meal an hour
earlier. A patient, who cannot touch his dinner at two,
will often accept it gladly, if brought to him at seven.
But somehow nurses never "think of these things." One
would imagine they did not consider themselves bound
to exercise their judgment; they leave it to the patient.
Now I am quite sure that it is better for a patient rather
to suffer these neglects than to try to teach his nurse to
nurse him, if she does not know how. It ruffles him, and
if he is ill he is in no condition to teach, especially upon

---

[8] Offending.

himself. The above remarks apply much more to private
nursing than to hospitals.

Nurse must have some rule of thought about her patient's diet

I would say to the nurse, have a rule of thought about
your patient's diet; consider, remember how much he
has had, and how much he ought to have today.
Generally, the only rule of the private patient's diet is
what the nurse has to give. It is true she cannot give him
what she has not got; but his stomach does not wait for
her convenience, or even her necessity[xxii]. If it is used to
having its stimulus at one hour today, and to-morrow it
does not have it, because she has failed in getting it, he
will suffer. She must be always exercising her ingenuity
to supply defects, and to remedy accidents which will
happen among the best contrivers, but from which the
patient does not suffer the less, because "they cannot be
helped."

Keep your patient's cup dry underneath

One very minute caution, — take care not to spill into
your patient's saucer, in other words, take care that the
outside bottom rim of his cup shall be quite dry and
clean; if, every time he lifts his cup to his lips, he has to
carry the saucer with it, or else to drop the liquid upon,
and to soil his sheet, or his bed gown, or pillow, or if he
is sitting up, his dress, you have no idea what a
difference this minute want of care on your part makes
to his comfort and even to his willingness for food.

VII. What Food?

Common errors in diet

I will mention one or two of the most common errors among women in charge of sick respecting sick diet. Beef tea. One is the belief that beef tea is the most nutritive of all articles. Now, just try and boil down a lb. of beef into beef tea, evaporate your beef tea, and see what is left of your beef. You will find that there is barely a teaspoonful of solid nourishment to half a pint of water in beef tea; — nevertheless there is a certain reparative quality in it, we do not know what, as there is in tea; — but it may safely be given in almost any inflammatory disease, and is as little to be depended upon with the healthy or convalescent where much nourishment is required. Again, it is an ever ready saw that an egg is equivalent to a lb. of meat, — whereas it is not at all so. Eggs. Also, it is seldom noticed with how many patients, particularly of nervous or bilious temperament, eggs disagree. All puddings made with eggs, are distasteful to them in consequence. An egg, whipped up with wine, is often the only form in which they can take this kind of nourishment. Meat without vegetables. Again, if the patient has attained to eating meat, it is supposed that to give him meat is the only thing needful for his recovery; whereas scorbutic sores have been actually known to appear among sick persons living in the midst of plenty in England, which could be traced to no other source than this, viz.: that the nurse, depending on meat alone, had allowed the patient to be without vegetables for a considerable time, these latter being so badly cooked that he always left them untouched. Arrowroot. Arrowroot is another grand dependence of the nurse. As a vehicle for wine, and as a restorative quickly prepared, it is all very well. But it is nothing but starch and water. Flour is both more nutritive, and less liable to ferment, and is preferable wherever it can be used.

Milk, butter, cream, etc.

Again, milk and the preparations from milk are a most important article of food for the sick. Butter is the lightest kind of animal fat, and though it wants the sugar and some of the other elements which there are in milk, yet it is most valuable both in itself and in enabling the patient to eat more bread. Flour, oats, groats[9], barley, and their kind, are as we have already said, preferable in all their preparations to all the preparations of arrow root, sago, tapioca, and their kind. Cream, in many long chronic diseases, is quite irreplaceable by any other article whatever. It seems to act in the same manner as beef tea, and to most it is much easier of digestion than milk. In fact, it seldom disagrees. Cheese is not usually digestible by the sick, but it is pure nourishment for repairing waste; and I have seen sick, and not a few either, whose craving for cheese showed how much it was needed by them[xxiii].

But, if fresh milk is so valuable a food for the sick, the least change or sourness in it, makes it of all articles, perhaps, the most injurious; diarrhea is a common result of fresh milk allowed to become at all sour. The nurse therefore ought to exercise her utmost care in this. In large institutions for the sick, even the poorest, the utmost care is exercised. Wenham Lake ice is used for this express purpose every summer, while the private patient, perhaps, never tastes a drop of milk that is not sour, all through the hot weather, so little does the private nurse understand the necessity of such care. Yet, if you consider that the only drop of real nourishment in your patient's tea is the drop of milk, and how much almost all English patients depend upon their tea, you

1.   [9] Hulled or crushed grain.

will see the great importance of not depriving your patient of this drop of milk. Buttermilk, a totally different thing, is often very useful, especially in fevers.

Sweet things

In laying down rules of diet, by the amounts of "solid nutriment" in different kinds of food, it is constantly lost sight of what the patient requires to repair his waste, what he can take and what he can't. You cannot diet a patient from a book, you cannot make up the human body as you would make up a prescription, — so many parts "carboniferous," so many parts "nitrogenous" will constitute a perfect diet for the patient. The nurse's observation here will materially assist the doctor — the patient's "fancies" will materially assist the nurse. For instance, sugar is one of the most nutritive of all articles, being pure carbon, and is particularly recommended in some books. But the vast majority of all patients in England, young and old, male and female, rich and poor, hospital and private, dislike sweet things, — and while I have never known a person take to sweets when he was ill who disliked them when he was well, I have known many fond of them when in health, who in sickness would leave off anything sweet, even to sugar in tea, — sweet puddings, sweet drinks, are their aversion; the furred tongue almost always likes what is sharp or pungent. Scorbutic patients are an exception; they often crave for sweetmeats and jams.

Jelly

Jelly is another article of diet in great favor with nurses and friends of the sick; even if it could be eaten solid, it would not nourish, but it is simply the height of folly to take $1/8$ oz. of gelatin and make it into a certain bulk by dissolving it in water and then to give it to the sick, as if the mere bulk represented nourishment. It is now known that jelly does not nourish, that it has a tendency to produce diarrhea, — and to trust to it to repair the waste of a diseased constitution is simply to starve the sick under the guise of feeding them. If 100 spoonfuls of jelly were given in the course of the day, you would have given one spoonful of gelatin, which spoonful has no nutritive power whatever.

And, nevertheless, gelatin contains a large quantity of nitrogen, which is one of the most powerful elements in nutrition; on the other hand, beef tea may be chosen as an illustration of great nutrient power in sickness, co-existing with a very small amount of solid nitrogenous matter.

Beef tea

Dr. Christison says that "everyone will be struck with the readiness with which" certain classes of "patients will often take diluted meat juice or beef tea repeatedly, when they refuse all other kinds of food." This is particularly remarkable in "cases of gastric fever, in which," he says, "little or nothing else besides beef tea or diluted meat juice" has been taken for weeks or even months, "and yet a pint of beef tea contains scarcely ¼ oz. of anything but water," — the result is so striking that he asks what is its mode of action? "Not simply nutrient — ¼ oz. of the most nutritive material cannot nearly replace the daily wear and tear of the tissues in any circumstances. Possibly," he says, "it belongs to a new denomination of remedies."

It has been observed that a small quantity of beef tea, added to other articles of nutrition augments their power out of all proportion to the additional amount of solid matter.

The reason why jelly should be innutritious and beef tea nutritious to the sick, is a secret yet undiscovered, but it clearly shows that careful observation of the sick is the only clue to the best dietary.

Observation, not chemistry, must decide sick diet

Chemistry has as yet afforded little insight into the dieting of sick. All that chemistry can tell us is the amount of "carboniferous" or "nitrogenous" elements discoverable in different dietetic articles. It has given us lists of dietetic substances, arranged in the order of their richness in one or other of these principles; but that is all. In the great majority of cases, the stomach of the patient is guided by other principles of selection than merely the amount of carbon or nitrogen in the diet. No doubt, in this as in other things, nature has very definite rules for her guidance, but these rules can only be ascertained by the most careful observation at the bed-side. She there teaches us that living chemistry, the chemistry of reparation, is something different from the chemistry of the laboratory. Organic chemistry is useful, as all knowledge is, when we come face to face with nature; but it by no means follows that we should learn in the laboratory any one of the reparative processes going on in disease.

Again, the nutritive power of milk and of the preparations from milk, is very much undervalued; there is nearly as much nourishment in half a pint of milk as there is in a quarter of a lb. of meat. But this is not the whole question or nearly the whole. The main question is what the patient's stomach can assimilate or derive nourishment from, and of this the patient's stomach is the sole judge. Chemistry cannot tell this. The patient's stomach must be its own chemist. The diet which will keep the healthy man healthy will kill the sick one. The same beef which is the most nutritive of all meat and which nourishes the healthy man is the least nourishing of all food to the sick man, whose half-dead stomach can *assimilate* no part of it, that is, make no food out of it. On a diet of beef tea healthy men on the other hand speedily lose their strength.

Home-made bread

I have known patients live for many months without touching bread, because they could not eat baker's bread. These were mostly country patients, but not all. Homemade bread or brown bread is a most important article of diet for many patients. The use of aperients may be entirely superseded by it. Oat cake is another.

Sound observation has scarcely yet been brought to bear on sick diet

To watch for the opinions, then, which the patient's stomach gives, rather than to read "analyses of foods," is the business of all those who have to settle what the patient is to eat — perhaps the most important thing to be provided for him after the air he is to breathe.

Now the medical man who sees the patient only once a day or even only once or twice a week, cannot possibly tell this without the assistance of the patient himself, or of those who are in constant observation on the patient. The utmost the medical man can tell is whether the patient is weaker or stronger at this visit than he was at the last visit. I should therefore say that incomparably the most important office of the nurse, after she has taken care of the patient's air, is to take care to observe the effect of his food, and report it to the medical attendant.

It is quite incalculable the good that would certainly come from such *sound* and close observation in this almost neglected branch of nursing, or the help it would give to the medical man.

Tea and coffee

A great deal too much against tea[xxiv] is said by wise people, and a great deal too much of tea is given to the sick by foolish people. When you see the natural and almost universal craving in English sick for their "tea," you cannot but feel that nature knows what she is about.

But a little tea or coffee restores them quite as much as a great deal, and a great deal of tea and especially of coffee impairs the little power of digestion they have. Yet a nurse because she sees how one or two cups of tea or coffee restores her patient, thinks that three or four cups will do twice as much. This is not the case at all; it is however certain that there is nothing yet discovered which is a substitute to the English patient for his cup of tea; he can take it when he can take nothing else, and he often can't take anything else if he has it not. I should be very glad if any of the abusers of tea would point out what to give to an English patient after a sleepless night, instead of tea. If you give it at 5 or 6 o'clock in the morning, he may even sometimes fall asleep after it, and get perhaps his only two or three hours' sleep during the twenty-four. At the same time you never should give tea or coffee to the sick, as a rule, after 5 o'clock in the afternoon. Sleeplessness in the early night is from excitement generally and is increased by tea or coffee; sleeplessness which continues to the early morning is from exhaustion often, and is relieved by tea. The only English patients I have ever known refuse tea, have been typhus cases, and the first sign of their getting better was their craving again for tea. In general, the dry and dirty tongue always prefers tea to coffee, and will quite decline milk, unless with tea. Coffee is a better restorative than tea, but a greater impairer of the digestion. Let the patient's taste decide. You will say that, in cases of great thirst, the patient's craving decides that it will drink *a great deal* of tea, and that you cannot help it. But in these cases be sure that the patient requires diluents for quite other purposes than quenching the thirst; he wants a great deal of some drink, not only of tea, and the doctor will order what he is to have, barley water or lemonade, or soda water and milk, as the case may be.

Lehmann, quoted by Dr. Christison, says that, among the well and active "the infusion of 1 oz. of roasted coffee daily will diminish the waste" going on in the body "by one-fourth," and Dr. Christison adds that tea has the same property. Now this is actual experiment. Lehmann weighs the man and finds the fact from his weight. It is not deduced from any "analysis" of food. All experience among the sick shows the same thing.[xxv]

Cocoa

Cocoa is often recommended to the sick in lieu of tea or coffee. But independently of the fact that English sick very generally dislike cocoa, it has quite a different effect from tea or coffee. It is an oily starchy nut having no restorative power at all, but simply increasing fat. It is pure mockery of the sick, therefore, to call it a substitute for tea.

Bulk

An almost universal error among nurses is in the bulk of the food and especially the drinks they offer to their patients. Suppose a patient ordered 4 oz. brandy during the day, how is he to take this if you make it into four pints with diluting it? The same with tea and beef tea, with arrowroot, milk, etc. You have not increased the nourishment, you have not increased the renovating power of these articles, by increasing their bulk, — you have very likely diminished both by giving the patient's digestion more to do, and most likely of all, the patient will leave half of what he has been ordered to take, because he cannot swallow the bulk with which you have been pleased to invest it. It requires very nice observation and care to determine what will not be too thick or strong for the patient to take, while giving him no more than the bulk which he is able to swallow.

VIII. Bed and Bedding

Feverishness a symptom of bedding

A few words upon bedsteads and bedding; and principally as regards patients who are entirely, or almost entirely, confined to bed.

Feverishness is generally supposed to be a symptom of fever — in nine cases out of ten it is a symptom of bedding.[xxvi] The patient has had reintroduced into the body the emanations from himself which day after day and week after week saturate his unaired bedding. How can it be otherwise? Look at the ordinary bed in which a patient lies.

Uncleanliness of ordinary bedding

If I were looking out for an example in order to show what *not* to do, I should take the specimen of an ordinary bed in a private house: a wooden bedstead, two or even three mattresses piled up to above the height of a table; a valance attached to the frame — nothing but a miracle could ever thoroughly dry or air such a bed and bedding. The patient must inevitably alternate between cold damp after his bed is made, and warm damp before, both saturated with organic matter,[xxvii] and this from the time the mattresses are put under him till the time they are picked to pieces, if this is ever done.

Air your dirty sheets, not only your clean ones

If you consider that an adult in health exhales by the lungs and skin in the twenty-four hours three pints at least of moisture, loaded with organic matter ready to enter into putrefaction; that in sickness the quantity is often greatly increased, the quality is always more noxious — just ask yourself next where does all this moisture go to? Chiefly into the bedding, because it cannot go anywhere else. And it stays there; because, except perhaps a weekly change of sheets, scarcely any other airing is attempted. A nurse will be careful to fidgetiness about airing the clean sheets from clean damp, but airing the dirty sheets from noxious damp will never even occur to her. Besides this, the most dangerous effluvia we know of are from the excreta of the sick — these are placed, at least temporarily, where they must throw their effluvia into the underside of the bed, and the space under the bed is never aired; it cannot be, with our arrangements. Must not such a bed be always saturated, and be always the means of re-introducing into the system of the unfortunate patient who lies in it, that excrementitiously matter to eliminate which from the body nature had expressly appointed the disease?

My heart always sinks within me when I hear the good housewife, of every class, say, "I assure you the bed has been well slept in," and I can only hope it is not true. What? is the bed already saturated with somebody else's damp before my patient comes to exhale into it his own damp? Has it not had a single chance to be aired? No, not one. "It has been slept in every night."

Iron spring bedstead the best

The only way of really nursing a real patient is to have an *iron* bedstead, with recline springs, which are permeable by the air up to the very mattress (no valance, of course), the mattress to be a thin hair one; the bed to be not above 3½ feet wide. Comfort and cleanliness of *two* beds. If the patient be entirely confined to his bed, there should be *two* such bedsteads; each bed to be "made" with mattress, sheets, blankets, etc., complete — the patient to pass twelve hours in each bed; on no account to carry his sheets with him. The whole of the bedding to be hung up to air for each intermediate twelve hours. Of course there are many cases where this cannot be done at all — many more where only an approach to it can be made. I am indicating the ideal of nursing, and what I have actually had done. But about the kind of bedstead there can be no doubt, whether there be one or two provided.

Bed not to be too wide

There is a prejudice in favor of a wide bed — I believe it to be a prejudice. All the refreshment of moving a patient from one side to the other of his bed is far more effectually secured by putting him into a fresh bed; and a patient who is really very ill does not stray far in bed. But it is said there is no room to put a tray down on a narrow bed. No good nurse will ever put a tray on a bed at all. If the patient can turn on his side, he will eat more comfortably from a bedside table; and on no account whatever should a bed ever be higher than a sofa. Otherwise the patient feels himself "out of humanity's reach"; he can get at nothing for himself: he can move nothing for himself. If the patient cannot turn, a table over the bed is a better thing. I need hardly say that a patient's bed should never have its side against the wall. The nurse must be able to get easily to both sides the bed and to reach easily every part of the patient without stretching — a thing impossible if the bed be either too wide or too high.

Bed not to be too high

When I see a patient in a room nine or ten feet high upon a bed between four and five feet high, with his head, when he is sitting up in bed, actually within two or three feet of the ceiling, I ask myself, is this expressly planned to produce that peculiarly distressing feeling common to the sick, viz., as if the walls and ceiling were closing in upon them, and they becoming sandwiches between floor and ceiling, which imagination is not, indeed, here so far from the truth? If, over and above this, the window stops short of the ceiling, then the patient's head may literally be raised above the stratum of fresh air, even when the window is open. Can human perversity any farther go, in unmaking the process of restoration which God has made? The fact is that the heads of sleepers or of sick should never be higher than the throat of the chimney, which ensures their being in the current of best air. And we will not suppose it possible that you have closed your chimney with a chimney-board.

If a bed is higher than a sofa, the difference of the fatigue of getting in and out of bed will just make the difference, very often, to the patient (who can get in and out of bed at all) of being able to take a few minutes' exercise, either in the open air or in another room. It is so very odd that people never think of this, or of how many more times a patient who is in bed for the twenty-four hours is obliged to get in and out of bed than they are, who only, it is to be hoped, get into bed once and out of bed once during the twenty-four hours. Nor in a dark place.

A patient's bed should always be in the lightest spot in the room; and he should be able to see out of window.

Nor a four poster with curtains

I need scarcely say that the old four-post bed with curtains is utterly inadmissible, whether for sick or well. Hospital bedsteads are in many respects very much less objectionable than private ones.

Scrofula often a result of disposition of bedclothes

There is reason to believe that not a few of the apparently unaccountable cases of scrofula among children proceed from the habit of sleeping with the head under the bed clothes, and so inhaling air already breathed, which is farther contaminated by exhalations from the skin. Patients are sometimes given to a similar habit, and it often happens that the bed clothes are so disposed that the patient must necessarily breathe air more or less contaminated by exhalations from his skin.

A good nurse will be careful to attend to this. It is an important part, so to speak, of ventilation.

Bedsores

It may be worthwhile to remark, that where there is any danger of bedsores a blanket should never be placed *under* the patient. It retains damp and acts like a poultice.

Heavy and impervious bedclothes

Never use anything but light Witney blankets as bed covering for the sick. The heavy cotton impervious counterpane[10] is bad, for the very reason that it keeps in the emanations from the sick person, while the blanket allows them to pass through. Weak patients are invariably distressed by a great weight of bed-clothes, which often prevents their getting any sound sleep whatever.

Note: — One word about pillows. Every weak patient, be his illness what it may, suffers more or less from difficulty in breathing. To take the weight of the body off the poor chest, which is hardly up to its work as it is, ought therefore to be the object of the nurse in arranging his pillows. Now what does she do and what are the consequences? She piles the pillows one a-top of the other like a wall of bricks. The head is thrown upon the chest. And the shoulders are pushed forward, so as not to allow the lungs room to expand. The pillows, in fact, lean upon the patient, not the patient upon the pillows. It is impossible to give a rule for this, because it must vary with the figure of the patient. And tall patients suffer much more than short ones, because of the *drag* of the long limbs upon the waist. But the object is to support, with the pillows, the back *below* the breathing apparatus, to allow the shoulders room to fall back, and to support the head, without throwing it forward. The suffering of dying patients is immensely increased by

---

[10] A bedspread.

neglect of these points. And many an invalid, too weak to drag about his pillows himself, slips his book or anything at hand behind the lower part of his back to support it.

IX. Light

Light essential to both health and recovery

It is the unqualified result of all my experience with the sick, that second only to their need of fresh air is their need of light; that, after a close room, what hurts them most is a dark room. And that it is not only light but direct sun-light they want. I had rather have the power of carrying my patient about after the sun, according to the aspect of the rooms, if circumstances permit, than let him linger in a room when the sun is off. People think the effect is upon the spirits only. This is by no means the case. The sun is not only a painter but a sculptor. You admit that he does the photograph. Without going into any scientific exposition we must admit that light has quite as real and tangible effects upon the human body. But this is not all. Who has not observed the purifying effect of light, and especially of direct sunlight, upon the air of a room? Here is an observation within everybody's experience. Go into a room where the shutters are always shut, (in a sick room or a bedroom there should never be shutters shut), and though the room be uninhabited, though the air has never been polluted by the breathing of human beings, you will observe a close, musty smell of corrupt air, of air *i.e.* unpurified by the effect of the sun's rays. The mustiness of dark rooms and corners, indeed, is proverbial. The cheerfulness of a room, the usefulness of light in treating disease is all-important.

Aspect, view and sunlight matters of first importance to the sick

A very high authority in hospital construction has said that people do not enough consider the difference between wards and dormitories in planning their buildings. But I go farther, and say, that healthy people never remember the difference between *bed*rooms and *sickrooms*, in making arrangements for the sick. To a sleeper in health it does not signify what the view is from his bed. He ought never to be in it excepting when asleep, and at night. Aspect does not very much signify either (provided the sun reach his bedroom some time in every day, to purify the air), because he ought never to be in his bedroom except during the hours when there is no sun. But the case is exactly reversed with the sick, even should they be as many hours out of their beds as you are in yours, which probably they are not. Therefore, that they should be able, without raising themselves or turning in bed, to see out of window from their beds, to see sky and sun-light at least, if you can show them nothing else, I assert to be, if not of the very first importance for recovery, at least something very near it. And you should therefore look to the position of the beds of your sick one of the very first things. If they can see out of two windows instead of one, so much the better. Again, the morning sun and the midday sun — the hours when they are quite certain not to be up, are of more importance to them, if a choice must be made, than the afternoon sun. Perhaps you can take them out of bed in the afternoon and set them by the window, where they can see the sun. But the best rule is, if possible, to give them direct sunlight from the moment he rises till the moment he sets.

Another great difference between the *bed*room and the *sickroom* is, that the *sleeper* has a very large balance of fresh air to begin with, when he begins the night, if his room has been open all day as it ought to be; the *sick* man has not, because all day he has been breathing the air in the same room, and dirtying it by the emanations from himself. Far more care is therefore necessary to keep up a constant change of air in the sick room.

It is hardly necessary to add that there are acute cases, (particularly a few ophthalmic cases, and diseases where the eye is morbidly sensitive), where a subdued light is necessary. But a dark north room is inadmissible even for these. You can always moderate the light by blinds and curtains.

Heavy, thick, dark window or bed curtains should, however, hardly ever be used for any kind of sick in this country. A light white curtain at the head of the bed is, in general, all that is necessary, and a green blind to the window, to be drawn down only when necessary.

Without sunlight, we degenerate body and mind

One of the greatest observers of human things (not physiological), says, in another language, "Where there is sun there is thought." All physiology goes to confirm this. Where is the shady side of deep valleys, there is cretinism[11]. Where are cellars and the not sunny sides of narrow streets, there is the degeneracy and weakness of the human race — mind and body equally degenerating. Put the pale withering plant and human being into the sun, and, if not too far gone, each will recover health and spirit.

Almost all patients lie with their faces to the light

It is a curious thing to observe how almost all patients lie with their faces turned to the light, exactly as plants always make their faces turned to the light; a patient will even complain that it gives him pain "lying on that side." "Then why *do* you lie on that side?" He does not know, — but we do. It is because it is the side towards the window. A fashionable physician has recently published in a government report that he always turns his patients' faces from the light. Yes, but nature is stronger than fashionable physicians, and depend upon it she turns the faces back and *towards* such light as she can get. Walk through the wards of a hospital, remember the bed sides of private patients you have

---

[11] A congenital condition caused by a deficiency of thyroid hormone.

seen, and count how many sick you ever saw lying with their faces towards the wall.

X. Cleanliness of Rooms and Walls

Cleanliness of carpets and furniture

It cannot be necessary to tell a nurse that she should be clean, or that she should keep her patient clean, — seeing that the greater part of nursing consists in preserving cleanliness. No ventilation can freshen a room or ward where the most scrupulous cleanliness is not observed. Unless the wind is blowing through the windows at the rate of twenty miles an hour, dusty carpets, dirty wainscots, musty curtains and furniture, will infallibly produce a close smell. I have lived in a large and expensively furnished London house, where the only constant inmate in two very lofty rooms, with opposite windows, was myself, and yet, owing to the abovementioned dirty circumstances, no opening of windows could ever keep those rooms free from closeness; but the carpet and curtains having been turned out of the rooms altogether, they became instantly as fresh as could be wished. It is pure nonsense to say that in London a room cannot be kept clean. Many of our hospitals show the exact reverse.

Dust never removed now

But no particle of dust is ever or can ever be removed or really got rid of by the present system of dusting. Dusting in these days means nothing but flapping the dust from one part of a room on to another with doors and windows closed. What you do it for I cannot think. You had much better leave the dust alone, if you are not going to take it away altogether. For from the time a room begins to be a room up to the time when it ceases to be one, no one atom of dust ever actually leaves its precincts. Tidying a room means nothing now but removing a thing from one place, which it has kept clean for itself, on to another and a dirtier one[xxviii]. Flapping by way of cleaning is only admissible in the case of pictures, or anything made of paper. The only way I know to *remove* dust, the plague of all lovers of fresh air, is to wipe everything with a damp cloth. And all furniture ought to be so made as that it may be wiped with a damp cloth without injury to itself, and so polished as that it may be damped without injury to others. To dust, as it is now practiced, truly means to distribute dust more equally over a room.

Floors

As to floors, the only really clean floor I know is the Berlin *lacquered* floor, which is wet rubbed and dry rubbed every morning to remove the dust. The French *parquet* is always more or less dusty, although infinitely superior in point of cleanliness and healthiness to our absorbent floor.

For a sick room, a carpet is perhaps the worst expedient which could by any possibility have been invented. If you must have a carpet, the only safety is to take it up two or three times a year, instead of once. A dirty carpet literally infects the room. And if you consider the enormous quantity of organic matter from the feet of people coming in, which must saturate it, this is by no means surprising.

Papered, plastered, oil-painted walls

As for walls, the worst is the papered wall; the next worst is plaster. But the plaster can be redeemed by frequent lime-washing; the paper requires frequent renewing. A glazed paper gets rid of a good deal of the danger. But the ordinary bedroom paper is all that it ought *not* to be[xxix].

The close connection between ventilation and cleanliness is shown in this. An ordinary light paper will last clean much longer if there is an Arnott's ventilator in the chimney than it otherwise would.

The best wall now extant is oil paint. From this you can wash the animal exuviæ.[xxx]

These are what make a room musty.

Best kind of wall for a sickroom.

The best wall for a sickroom or ward that could be made is pure white non-absorbent cement or glass, or glazed tiles, if they were made slightly enough.

Air can be soiled just like water. If you blow into water you will soil it with the animal matter from your breath. So it is with air. Air is always soiled in a room where walls and carpets are saturated with animal exhalations.

Want of cleanliness, then, in rooms and wards, which you have to guard against, may arise in three ways.

Dirty air from without

1. Dirty air coming in from without, soiled by sewer emanations, the evaporation from dirty streets, smoke, bits of un-burnt fuel, bits of straw, bits of horse dung.

    Best kind of wall for a house.

    If people would but cover the outside walls of their houses with plain or encaustic tiles, what an incalculable improvement would there be in light, cleanliness, dryness, warmth, and consequently economy. The play of a fire engine would then effectually wash the outside of a house. This kind of *walling* would stand next to paving in improving the health of towns.

2. Dirty air coming from within, from dust, which you often displace, but never remove. And this recalls what ought to be a *sine qua non*. Have as few ledges in your room or ward as possible. And under no presence have any ledge whatever out of sight. Dust accumulates there, and will never be wiped off. This is a certain way to soil the air. Besides this, the

animal exhalations from your inmates saturate your furniture. And if you never clean your furniture properly, how can your rooms or wards be anything but musty? Ventilate as you please, the rooms will never be sweet. Besides this, there is a constant *degradation*, as it is called taking place from everything except polished or glazed articles — *E.g.*, in coloring certain green papers arsenic is used. Now in the very dust even, which is lying about in rooms hung with this kind of green paper, arsenic has been distinctly detected. You see your dust is anything but harmless; yet you will let such dust lie about your ledges for months, your rooms for ever.

Again, the fire fills the room with coal dust.

3. Dirty air coming from the carpet. Above all, take care of the carpets that the animal dirt left there by the feet of visitors does not stay there. Floors, unless the grain is filled up and polished, are just as bad. The smell from the floor of a schoolroom or ward, when any moisture brings out the organic matter by which it is saturated, might alone be enough to warn us of the mischief that is going on.

Remedies

The outer air, then, can only be kept clean by sanitary improvements, and by consuming smoke. The expense in soap, which this single improvement would save, is quite incalculable.

The inside air can only be kept clean by excessive care in the ways mentioned above — to rid the walls, carpets, furniture, ledges, etc., of the organic matter and dust — dust consisting greatly of this organic matter— with which they become saturated, and which is what really makes the room musty.

Without cleanliness, you cannot have all the effect of ventilation; without ventilation, you can have no thorough cleanliness.

Very few people, be they of what class they may, have any idea of the exquisite cleanliness required in the sickroom. For much of what I have said applies less to the hospital than to the private sickroom. The smoky chimney, the dusty furniture, the utensils emptied but once a day, often keeps the air of the sick constantly dirty in the best private houses.

The well have a curious habit of forgetting that what is to them but a trifling inconvenience, to be patiently "put up" with, is to the sick a source of suffering, delaying recovery, if not actually hastening death. The wells are scarcely ever more than eight hours, at most, in the same room. Some change they can always make, if only for a few minutes. Even during the supposed eight hours, they can change their posture or their position in the room. But the sick man, who never leaves his bed, who cannot change by any movement of his own his air, or his light, or his warmth; who cannot obtain quiet, or get out of the smoke, or the smell, or the dust; he is really poisoned or depressed by what is to you the merest trifle.

"What can't be cured must be endured," is the very worst and most dangerous maxim for a nurse which ever was made. Patience and resignation in her are but other words for carelessness or indifference — contemptible, if in regard to herself; culpable, if in regard to her sick.

XI. Personal Cleanliness
Poisoning by the skin

In almost all diseases, the function of the skin is, more or less, disordered; and in many most important diseases nature relieves herself almost entirely by the skin. This is particularly the case with children. But the excretion, which comes from the skin, is left there, unless removed by washing or by the clothes. Every nurse should keep this fact constantly in mind, — for, if she allow her sick to remain unwashed, or their clothing to remain on them after being saturated with perspiration or other excretion, she is interfering injuriously with the natural processes of health just as effectually as if she were to give the patient a dose of slow poison by the mouth. Poisoning by the skin is no less certain than poisoning by the mouth — only it is slower in its operation.

Ventilation and skin-cleanliness equally essential

The amount of relief and comfort experienced by sick after the skin has been carefully washed and dried, is one of the commonest observations made at a sick bed. But it must not be forgotten that the comfort and relief so obtained are not all. They are, in fact, nothing more than a sign that the vital powers have been relieved by removing something that was oppressing them. The nurse, therefore, must never put off attending to the personal cleanliness of her patient under the plea that all that is to be gained is a little relief, which can be quite as well given later.

In all well regulated hospitals this ought to be, and generally is, attended to. But it is very generally neglected with private sick.

Just as it is necessary to renew the air round a sick person frequently, to carry off morbid effluvia from the lungs and skin, by maintaining free ventilation, so is it necessary to keep the pores of the skin free from all obstructing excretions. The object, both of ventilation and of skin-cleanliness, is pretty much the same, to wit, removing noxious matter from the system as rapidly as possible.

Care should be taken in all these operations of sponging, washing, and cleansing the skin, not to expose too great a surface at once, so as to check the perspiration, which would renew the evil in another form.

The various ways of washing the sick need not here be specified, — the less so as the doctors ought to say which is to be used.

In several forms of diarrhea, dysentery, etc., where the skin is hard and harsh, the relief afforded by washing with a great deal of soft soap is incalculable. In other cases, sponging with tepid soap and water, then with tepid water and drying with a hot towel will be ordered.

Every nurse ought to be careful to wash her hands very frequently during the day. If her face too, so much the better.

One word as to cleanliness merely as cleanliness.

Steaming and rubbing the skin

Compare the dirtiness of the water in which you have washed when it is cold without soap, cold with soap, hot with soap. You will find the first has hardly removed any dirt at all, the second a little more; the third a great deal more. But hold your hand over a cup of hot water for a minute or two, and then, by merely rubbing with the finger, you will bring off flakes of dirt or dirty skin. After a vapor bath you may peel your whole self-clean in this way. What I mean is, that by simply washing or sponging with water you do not really clean your skin. Take a rough towel, dip one corner in very hot water, — if a little spirit be added to it it will be more effectual, — and then rub as if you were rubbing the towel into your skin with your fingers. The black flakes which will come off will convince you that you were not clean before, however much soap and water you have used. These flakes are what require removing. And you can really keep yourself cleaner with a tumbler of hot water and a rough towel and rubbing, than with a whole apparatus of bath and soap and sponge, without rubbing. It is quite nonsense to say that anybody need be dirty. Patients have been kept as clean by these means on a long voyage, when a basin full of water could not be afforded, and when they could not be moved out of their berths, as if all the appurtenances of home had been at hand.

Washing, however, with a large quantity of water has quite other effects than those of mere cleanliness. The skin absorbs the water and becomes softer and more perspirable. To wash with soap and soft water is, therefore, desirable from other points of view than that of cleanliness.

XII. Chattering Hopes and Advices
Advising the sick
The sick man to his advisers:

"My advisers! Their name is legion. * * * Somehow or other, it seems a provision of the universal destinies, that every man, woman, and child should consider him, her, or itself privileged especially to advise me. Why? That is precisely what I want to know." And this is what I have to say to them. I have been advised to go to every place extant in and out of England—to take every kind of exercise by every kind of cart, carriage — yes, and even swing (!) and dumb-bell (!) in existence; to imbibe every different kind of stimulus that ever has been invented. And this when those *best* fitted to know, viz., medical men, after long and close attendance, had declared any journey out of the question, had prohibited any kind of motion whatever, had closely laid down the diet and drink. What would my advisers say, were they the medical attendants, and I the patient left their advice, and took the casual adviser's? But the singularity in Legion's mind is this: it never occurs to him that everybody else is doing the same thing, and that I the patient *must* perforce say, in sheer self-defense, like Rosalind, "I could not do with all."

Chattering hopes the bane of the sick
"Chattering Hopes" may seem an odd heading. But I really believe there is scarcely a greater worry which invalids have to endure than the incurable hopes of their friends. There is no one practice against which I can speak more strongly from actual personal experience, wide and long, of its effects during sickness observed both upon others and upon myself. I would appeal most seriously to all friends, visitors, and attendants of the sick to leave off this practice of attempting to "cheer"

the sick by making light of their danger and by exaggerating their probabilities of recovery.

Far more now than formerly does the medical attendant tell the truth to the sick who are really desirous to hear it about their own state.

How intense is the folly, then, to say the least of it, of the friend, be he even a medical man, who thinks that his opinion, given after a cursory observation, will weigh with the patient, against the opinion of the medical attendant, given, perhaps, after years of observation, after using every help to diagnosis afforded by the stethoscope, the examination of pulse, tongue, etc.; and certainly after much more observation than the friend can possibly have had.

Supposing the patient to be possessed of common sense, — how can the "favorable" opinion, if it is to be called an opinion at all, of the casual visitor "cheer" him, — when different from that of the experienced attendant? Unquestionably the latter may, and often does, turn out to be wrong. But which is most likely to be wrong?

Patient does not want to talk of himself

The fact is, that the patient[xxxi] is not "cheered" at all by these well-meaning, most tiresome friends. On the contrary, he is depressed and wearied. If, on the one hand, he exerts himself to tell each successive member of this too numerous conspiracy, whose name is legion, why he does not think as they do, — in what respect he is worse,—what symptoms exist that they know nothing of, — he is fatigued instead of "cheered," and his attention is fixed upon himself. In general, patients who are really ill do not want to talk about themselves. Hypochondriacs do, but again I say we are not on the subject of hypochondriacs.

Absurd consolations put forth for the benefit of the sick

If, on the other hand, and which is much more frequently the case, the patient says nothing, but the Shakespearian "Oh!" "Ah!" "Go to!" and "In good sooth!" in order to escape from the conversation about himself the sooner, he is depressed by want of sympathy. He feels isolated in the midst of friends. He feels what a convenience it would be, if there were any single person to whom he could speak simply and openly, without pulling the string upon himself of this shower-bath of silly hopes and encouragements; to whom he could express his wishes and directions without that person persisting in saying "I hope that it will please God yet to give you twenty years," or, "You have a long life of activity before you." How often we see at the end of biographies or of cases recorded in medical papers, "after a long illness A. died rather suddenly," or, "unexpectedly both to himself and to others." "Unexpectedly" to others, perhaps, who did not see, because they did not look; but by no means "unexpectedly to himself," as I feel entitled to believe, both from the internal evidence in such stories, and from watching similar cases: there was every reason to expect that A. would die, and he knew it; but he found it useless to insist upon his own knowledge to his friends.

In these remarks I am alluding neither to acute cases which terminate rapidly nor to "nervous" cases.

By the first much interest in their own danger is very rarely felt. In writings of fiction, whether novels or biographies, these deathbeds are generally depicted as almost seraphic in lucidity of intelligence. Sadly large has been my experience in deathbeds, and I can only say that I have seldom or never seen such. Indifference, excepting with regard to bodily suffering, or to some duty the dying man desires to perform, is the far more usual state.

The "nervous case," on the other hand, delights in figuring to himself and others a fictitious danger.

But the long chronic case, who knows too well himself, and who has been told by his physician that he will never enter active life again, who feels that every month he has to give up something he could do the month before — oh! spare such sufferers your chattering hopes. You do not know how you worry and weary them. Such real sufferers cannot bear to talk of themselves, still less to hope for what they cannot at all expect.

So also as to all the advice showered so profusely upon such sick, to leave off some occupation, to try some other doctor, some other house, climate, pill, powder, or specific; I say nothing of the inconsistency — for these advisers are sure to be the same persons who exhorted the sick man not to believe his own doctor's prognostics, because "doctors are always mistaken," but to believe some other doctor, because "this doctor is always right." Sure also are these advisers to be the persons to bring the sick man fresh occupation, while exhorting him to leave his own.

Wonderful presumption of the advisers of the sick

Wonderful is the face with which friends, lay and medical, will come in and worry the patient with recommendations to do something or other, having just as little knowledge as to its being feasible, or even safe for him, as if they were to recommend a man to take exercise, not knowing he had broken his leg. What would the friend say, if *he* were the medical attendant, and if the patient, because some *other* friend had come in, because somebody, anybody, nobody, had recommended something, anything, nothing, were to disregard *his* orders, and take that other body's recommendation? But people never think of this.

Advisers the same now as two hundred years ago

A celebrated historical personage has related the commonplaces which, when on the eve of executing a remarkable resolution, were showered in nearly the same words by everyone around successively for a period of six months. To these the personage states that it was found least trouble always to reply the same thing, viz., that it could not be supposed that such a resolution had been taken without sufficient previous consideration. To patients enduring every day for years from every friend or acquaintance, either by letter or *vivâ voce*[12], some torment of this kind, I would suggest the same answer. It would indeed be spared, if such friends and acquaintances would but consider for one moment, that it is probable the patient has heard such advice at least fifty times before, and that, had it been practicable, it would have been practiced long ago. But of such consideration there appears to be no chance. Strange, though true, that people should be just the same in these things as they were a few hundred years ago!

To me these commonplaces, leaving their smear upon the cheerful, single-hearted, constant devotion to duty, which is so often seen in the decline of such sufferers, recall the slimy trail left by the snail on the sunny southern garden-wall loaded with fruit.

Mockery of the advice given to sick

No mockery in the world is so hollow as the advice showered upon the sick. It is of no use for the sick to say anything, for what the adviser wants is, *not* to know the truth about the state of the patient, but to turn whatever the sick may say to the support of his own argument, set forth, it must be repeated, without any inquiry whatever into the patient's real condition. "But it would be impertinent or indecent in me to make such an

---

[12] Orally rather than in writing.

inquiry," says the adviser. True; and how much more impertinent is it to give your advice when you can know nothing about the truth, and admit you could not inquire into it.

To nurses I say — these are the visitors who do your patient harm. When you hear him told:

1. That he has nothing the matter with him, and that he wants cheering.
2. That he is committing suicide, and that he wants preventing.
3. That he is the tool of somebody who makes use of him for a purpose.
4. That he will listen to nobody, but is obstinately bent upon his own way; and
5. That he ought to be called to the sense of duty, and is flying in the face of Providence; — then know that your patient is receiving all the injury that he can receive from a visitor.

How little the real sufferings of illness are known or understood. How little does anyone in good health fancy him or even *her*self into the life of a sick person.

Means of giving pleasure to the sick

Do, you who are about the sick or who visit the sick try and give them pleasure, remember to tell them what will do so. How often in such visits the sick person has to do the whole conversation, exerting his own imagination and memory, while you would take the visitor, absorbed in his own anxieties, making no effort of memory or imagination, for the sick person. "Oh! my dear, I have so much to think of, I really quite forgot to tell him that; besides, I thought he would know it," says the visitor to another friend. How could "he know it"? Depend upon it, the people who say this are really those who have little "to think of." There are many burthened with business who always manage to keep a pigeonhole in their minds, full of things to tell the "invalid."

I do not say, don't tell him your anxieties — I believe it is good for him and good for you too; but if you tell him what is anxious, surely you can remember to tell him what is pleasant too.

A sick person does so enjoy hearing good news: — for instance, of a love and courtship, while in progress to a good ending. If you tell him only when the marriage takes place, he loses half the pleasure, which God knows he has little enough of; and ten to one but you have told him of some love-making with a bad ending.

A sick person also intensely enjoys hearing of any *material* good, any positive or practical success of the right. He has so much of books and fiction, of principles, and precepts, and theories; do, instead of advising him with advice he has heard at least fifty times before, tell him of one benevolent act which has really succeeded practically, — it is like a day's health to him.[xxxii]

You have no idea what the craving of sick with undiminished power of thinking, but little power of doing, is to hear of good practical action, when they can no longer partake in it.

Do observe these things with the sick. Do remember how their life is to them disappointed and incomplete. You see them lying there with miserable disappointments, from which they can have no escape but death, and you can't remember to tell them of what would give them so much pleasure, or at least an hour's variety.

They don't want you to be lachrymose and whining with them, they like you to be fresh and active and interested, but they cannot bear absence of mind, and they are so tired of the advice and preaching they receive from every body, no matter whom it is, they see.

There is no better society than babies and sick people for one another. Of course you must manage this so that neither shall suffer from it, which is perfectly possible. If you think the "air of the sickroom" bad for the baby, why it is bad for the invalid too, and, therefore, you will of course correct it for both. It freshens up a sick person's whole mental atmosphere to see "the baby." And a very young child, if unspoiled, will generally adapt itself wonderfully to the ways of a sick person, if the time they spend together is not too long.

If you knew how unreasonably sick people suffer from reasonable causes of distress, you would take more pains about all these things. An infant laid upon the sick bed will do the sick person, thus suffering, better than all your logic. A piece of good news will do the same. Perhaps you are afraid of "disturbing" him. You say there is no comfort for his present cause of affliction. It is perfectly reasonable. The distinction is this, if he is obliged to act, do not "disturb" him with another subject of thought just yet; help him to do what he wants to do: but, if he *has* done this, or if nothing *can* be done, then "disturb" him by all means. You will relieve, more effectually, unreasonable suffering from reasonable causes by telling him "the news," showing him "the baby," or giving him something new to think of or to look at than by all the logic in the world.

It has been very justly said that the sick are like children in this, that there is no *proportion* in events to them. Now it is your business as their visitor to restore this right proportion for them — to show them what the rest of the world is doing. How can they find it out otherwise? You will find them far more open to conviction than children in this. And you will find that their unreasonable intensity of suffering from unkindness, from want of sympathy, etc., will disappear with their freshened interest in the big world's events. But then you must be able to give them real interests, not gossip.

Two new classes of patients peculiar to this generation

Note: — There are two classes of patients which are unfortunately becoming more common every day, especially among women of the richer orders, to whom all these remarks are pre-eminently inapplicable.

1. Those who make health an excuse for doing nothing and at the same time allege that the being able to do nothing is their only grief.
2. Those who have brought upon themselves ill-health by over pursuit of amusement, which they and their friends have most unhappily called intellectual activity. I scarcely know a greater injury that can be inflicted than the advice too often given to the first class "to vegetate" — or than the admiration too often bestowed on the latter class for "pluck."

XIII. Observation of the Sick

What is the use of the question, Is he better?

There is no sillier or universal question scarcely asked than this, "Is he better?" Ask it of the medical attendant, if you please. But of whom else, if you wish for a real answer to your question, would you ask it? Certainly not of the casual visitor; certainly not of the nurse, while the nurse's observation is so little exercised as it is now. What you want are facts, not opinions — for who can have any opinion of any value as to whether the patient is better or worse, excepting the constant medical attendant, or the really observing nurse?

The most important practical lesson that can be given to nurses is to teach them what to observe — how to observe — what symptoms indicate improvement — what the reverse — which are of importance — which are of none — which are the evidence of neglect — and of what kind of neglect.

All this is what ought to make part, and an essential part, of the training of every nurse. At present how few there are, either professional or unprofessional, who really know at all whether any sick person they may be with is better or worse.

The vagueness and looseness of the information one receives in answer to that much abused question, "Is he better?" would be ludicrous, if it were not painful. The only sensible answer (in the present state of knowledge about sickness) would be "How can I know? I cannot tell how he was when I was not with him."

I can record but a very few specimens of the answers[xxxiii] which I have heard made by friends and nurses, and accepted by physicians and surgeons at the very bedside of the patient, who could have contradicted every word, but did not — sometimes from amiability, often from shyness, oftenest from languor[13]!

"How often have the bowels acted, nurse?" "Once, sir."
This generally means that the utensil has been emptied
once, it having been used perhaps seven or eight times.

"Do you think the patient is much weaker than he was
six weeks ago?" "Oh no, sir; you know it is very long
since he has been up and dressed, and he can get across
the room now." This means that the nurse has not
observed that whereas six weeks ago he sat up and
occupied himself in bed, he now lies still doing nothing;
that, although he can "get across the room," he cannot
stand for five seconds.

Another patient who is eating well, recovering steadily,
although slowly, from a fever, but cannot walk or stand,
is represented to the doctor as making no progress at all.

Leading questions useless or misleading

Questions, too, as asked now (but too generally) of or
about patients, would obtain no information at all about
them, even if the person asked of had every information
to give. The question is generally a leading question;
and it is singular that people never think what must be
the answer to this question before they ask it: for
instance, "Has he had a good night?" Now, one patient
will think he has a bad night if he has not slept ten hours
without waking. Another does not think he has a bad
night if he has had intervals of dosing occasionally. The
same answer has actually been given as regarded two
patients — one who had been entirely sleepless for five
times twenty-four hours, and died of it, and another who
had not slept the sleep of a regular night, without
waking. Why cannot the question be asked, How many
hours' sleep has — had? and at what hours of the night?[xxxiv]
"I have never closed my eyes all night," an answer as
frequently made when the speaker has had several
hours' sleep as when he has had none, would then be

---

[13] The state or feeling, often pleasant, of tiredness or inertia.

less often said. Lies, intentional and unintentional, are much seldom told in answer to precise than to leading questions. Another frequent error is to inquire whether one cause remains, and not whether the effect which may be produced by a great many different causes, *not* inquired after, remains. As when it is asked, whether there was noise in the street last night; and if there were not, the patient is reported, without more ado, to have had a good night. Patients are completely taken aback by these kinds of leading questions, and give only the exact amount of information asked for, even when they know it to be completely misleading. The shyness of patients is seldom allowed for.

How few there are who, by five or six pointed questions, can elicit the whole case and get accurately to know and to be able to report *where* the patient is.

Means of obtaining inaccurate information

I knew a very clever physician, of large dispensary and hospital practice, who invariably began his examination of each patient with "Put your finger where you be bad." That man would never waste his time with collecting inaccurate information from nurse or patient. Leading questions always collect inaccurate information.

At a recent celebrated trial, the following leading question was put successively to nine distinguished medical men. "Can you attribute these symptoms to anything else but poison?" And out of the nine, eight answered "No!" without any qualification whatever. It appeared, upon cross-examination:

1. That none of them had ever seen a case of the kind of poisoning supposed.
2. That none of them had ever seen a case of the kind of disease to which the death, if not to poison, was attributable.

3. That none of them were even aware of the main fact of the disease and condition to which the death was attributable.

Surely nothing stronger can be adduced to prove what use leading questions are of, and what they lead to.

I had rather not say how many instances I have known, where, owing to this system of leading questions, the patient has died, and the attendants have been actually unaware of the principal feature of the case.

As to food patient takes or does not take

It is useless to go through all the particulars, besides sleep, in which people have a peculiar talent for gleaning inaccurate information. As to food, for instance, I often think that most common question, How is your appetite? can only be put because the questioner believes the questioned has really nothing the matter with him, which is very often the case. But where there is, the remark holds good which has been made about sleep. The *same* answer will often be made as regards a patient who cannot take two ounces of solid food per diem, and a patient who does not enjoy five meals a day as much as usual.

Again, the question, How is your appetite? is often put when How is your digestion? is the question meant. No doubt the two things depend on one another. But they are quite different. Many a patient can eat, if you can only "tempt his appetite." The fault lies in your not having got him the thing that he fancies. But many another patients do not care between grapes and turnips,—everything is equally distasteful to him. He would try to eat anything which would do him good; but everything "makes him worse." The fault here generally lies in the cooking. It is not his "appetite" which requires "tempting," it is his digestion which requires sparing. And good sick cookery will save the digestion half its work.

There may be four different causes, any one of which will produce the same result, viz., the patient slowly starving to death from want of nutrition:
1. Defect in cooking;
2. Defect in choice of diet;
3. Defect in choice of hours for taking diet;
4. Defect of appetite in patient.

Yet all these are generally comprehended in the one sweeping assertion that the patient has "no appetite."

Surely many lives might be saved by drawing a closer distinction; for the remedies are as diverse as the causes. The remedy for the first is, to cook better; for the second, to choose other articles of diet; for the third, to watch for the hours when the patient is in want of food; for the fourth, to show him what he likes, and sometimes unexpectedly. But no one of these remedies will do for any other of the defects not corresponding with it.

I cannot too often repeat that patients are generally either too languid to observe these things, or too shy to speak about them; nor is it well that they should be made to observe them, it fixes their attention upon themselves.

Again, I say, what *is* the nurse or friend there for except to take note of these things, instead of the patient doing so?[xxxv]

As to diarrhea

Again, the question is sometimes put, Is there diarrhea? And the answer will be the same, whether it is just merging into cholera, whether it is a trifling degree brought on by some trifling indiscretion, which will cease the moment the cause is removed, or whether there is no diarrhea at all, but simply relaxed bowels.

It is useless to multiply instances of this kind. As long as observation is so little cultivated as it is now, I do believe that it is better for the physician *not* to see the friends of the patient at all. They will oftener mislead him than not. And as often by making the patient out worse as better than he really is.

In the case of infants, *everything* must depend upon the accurate observation of the nurse or mother who has to report. And how seldom is this condition of accuracy fulfilled.

Means of cultivating sound and ready observation

A celebrated man, though celebrated only for foolish things, has told us that one of his main objects in the education of his son, was to give him a ready habit of accurate observation, a certainty of perception, and that for this purpose one of his means was a month's course as follows: — he took the boy rapidly past a toyshop; the father and son then described to each other as many of the objects as they could, which they had seen in passing the windows, noting them down with pencil and paper, and returning afterwards to verify their own accuracy. The boy always succeeded best, *e.g.*, if the father described 30 objects, the boy did 40, and scarcely ever made a mistake.

I have often thought how wise a piece of education this would be for much higher objects; and in our calling of nurses the thing itself is essential. For it may safely be said, not that the habit of ready and correct observation will by itself make us useful nurses, but that without it we shall be useless with all our devotion.

I have known a nurse in charge of a set of wards who not only carried in her head all the little varieties in the diets which each patient was allowed to fix for himself, but also exactly what each patient had taken during each day. I have known another nurse in charge of one single patient, who took away his meals day after day all but untouched, and never knew it.

If you find it helps you to note down such things on a bit of paper, in pencil, by all means do so. I think it more often lames than strengthens the memory and observation. But if you cannot get the habit of observation one way or other, you had better give up the being a nurse, for it is not your calling, however kind and anxious you may be.

Surely you can learn at least to judge with the eye how much an oz. of solid food is, how much an oz. of liquid. You will find this helps your observation and memory very much, you will then say to yourself "A. took about an oz. of his meat to day;" "B. took three times in 24 hours about ¼ pint of beef tea;" instead of saying "B. has taken nothing all day," or "I gave A. his dinner as usual."

Sound and ready observation essential in a nurse

I have known several of our real old-fashioned hospital "sisters," who could, as accurately as a measuring glass, measure out all their patients' wine and medicine by the eye, and never be wrong. I do not recommend this, one must be very sure of one's self to do it. I only mention it, because if a nurse can by practice measure medicine by the eye, surely she is no nurse who cannot measure by the eye about how much food (in oz.) her patient has taken.[xxxvi] In hospitals those who cut up the diets give with quite sufficient accuracy, to each patient, his 12 oz. or his 6 oz. of meat without weighing. Yet a nurse will often have patients loathing all food and incapable of any will to get well, who just tumble over the contents of the plate or dip the spoon in the cup to deceive the nurse, and she will take it away without ever seeing that there is just the same quantity of food as when she brought it, and she will tell the doctor, too, that the patient has eaten all his diets as usual, when all she ought to have meant is that she has taken away his diets as usual.

Now what kind of a nurse is this?

Difference of excitable and *accumulative* temperaments

I would call attention to something else, in which nurses frequently fail in observation. There is a well-marked distinction between the excitable and what I will call the *accumulative* temperament in patients. One will blaze up at once, under any shock or anxiety, and sleep very comfortably after it; another will seem quite calm and even torpid, under the same shock, and people say, "He hardly felt it at all," yet you will find him some time after slowly sinking. The same remark applies to the action of narcotics, of aperients, which, in the one, take effect directly, in the other not perhaps for twenty-four hours. A journey, a visit, an unwonted exertion, will affect the one immediately, but he recovers after it; the other bears it very well at the time, apparently, and dies or is prostrated for life by it. People often say how difficult the excitable temperament is to manage. I say how difficult is the *accumulative* temperament. With the first you have an outbreak which you could anticipate, and it is all over. With the second you never know where you are — you never know when the consequences are over. And it requires your closest observation to know what *are* the consequences of what — for the consequent by no means follows immediately upon the antecedent — and coarse observation is utterly at fault.

Superstition the fruit of bad observation

Almost all superstitions are owing to bad observation, to the *post hoc, ergo propter hoc*; and bad observers are almost all superstitious. Farmers used to attribute disease among cattle to witchcraft; weddings have been attributed to seeing one magpie, deaths to seeing three; and I have heard the most highly educated now-a-days draw consequences for the sick closely resembling these.

Physiognomy of disease little shown by the face

Another remark: although there is unquestionably a physiognomy of disease as well as of health; of all parts of the body, the face is perhaps the one which tells the least to the common observer or the casual visitor. Because, of all parts of the body, it is one most exposed to other influences, besides health. And people never, or scarcely ever, observe enough to know how to distinguish between the effect of exposure, of robust health, of a tender skin, of a tendency to congestion, of suffusion, flushing, or many other things. Again, the face is often the last to show emaciation. I should say that the hand was a much surer test than the face, both as to flesh, color, circulation, etc., etc. It is true that there are *some* diseases which are only betrayed at all by something in the face, *e.g.*, the eye or the tongue, as great irritability of brain by the appearance of the pupil of the eye. But we are talking of casual, not minute, observation. And few minute observers will hesitate to say that far more untruth than truth is conveyed by the oft repeated words, He *looks* well, or ill, or better or worse.

Wonderful is the way in which people will go upon the slightest observation, or often upon no observation at all, or upon some *saw* which the world's experience, if it had any, would have pronounced utterly false long ago.

I have known patients dying of sheer pain, exhaustion, and want of sleep, from one of the most lingering and painful diseases known, preserve, till within a few days of death, not only the healthy color of the cheek, but the mottled appearance of a robust child. And scores of times have I heard these unfortunate creatures assailed with, "I am glad to see you looking so well." "I see no reason why you should not live till ninety years of age." "Why don't you take a little more exercise and amusement?" with all the other commonplaces with which we are so familiar.

There is, unquestionably, a physiognomy of disease. Let the nurse learn it.

The experienced nurse can always tell that a person has taken a narcotic the night before by the patchiness of the color about the face, when the re-action of depression has set in; that very color which the inexperienced will point to as a proof of health.

There is, again, a faintness, which does not betray itself by the color at all, or in which the patient becomes brown instead of white. There is a faintness of another kind which, it is true, can always be seen by the paleness.

But the nurse seldom distinguishes. She will talk to the patient who is too faint to move, without the least scruple, unless he is pale and unless, luckily for him, the muscles of the throat are affected and he loses his voice.

Yet these two faintness's are perfectly distinguishable, by the mere countenance of the patient.

Peculiarities of patients

Again, the nurse must distinguish between the idiosyncrasies of patients. One likes to suffer out all his suffering alone, to be as little looked after as possible. Another likes to be perpetually made much of and pitied, and to have someone always by him. Both these peculiarities might be observed and indulged much more than they are. For quite as often does it happen that a busy attendance is forced upon the first patient, who wishes for nothing but to be "let alone," as that the second is left to think himself neglected.

Nurse must observe for herself increase of patient's weakness, patient will not tell her.

Again, I think that few things press so heavily on one suffering from long and incurable illness, as the necessity of recording in words from time to time, for the information of the nurse, who will not otherwise see, that he cannot do this or that, which he could do a month or a year ago. What is a nurse there for if she cannot observe these things for herself? Yet I have known — and known too among those — and *chiefly* among those — whom money and position put in possession of everything which money and position could give — I have known, I say, more accidents, (fatal, slowly or rapidly,) arising from this want of observation among nurses than from almost anything else. Because a patient could get out of a warm bath alone a month ago — because a patient could walk as far as his bell a week ago, the nurse concludes that he can do so now. She has never observed the change; and the patient is lost from being left in a helpless state of exhaustion, till someone accidentally comes in. And this not from any unexpected apoplectic, paralytic, or fainting fit (though even these could be expected far more, at least, than they are now, if we did but *observe*). No, from the expected, or to be expected, inevitable, visible, calculable, uninterrupted increase of weakness, which none need fail to observe.

Accidents arising from the nurse's want of observation.

Again, a patient not usually confined to bed, is compelled by an attack of diarrhea, vomiting, or other accident, to keep his bed for a few days; he gets up for the first time, and the nurse lets him go into another room, without coming in, a few minutes afterwards, to look after him. It never occurs to her that he is quite certain to be faint, or cold, or to want something. She says, as her excuse, Oh, he does not like to be fidgeted after. Yes, he said so some weeks ago; but he never said he did not like to be "fidgeted after," when he is in the state he is in now; and if he did, you ought to make some excuse to go in to him. More patients have been lost in this way than is at all generally known, viz., from relapses brought on by being left for an hour or two faint, or cold, or hungry, after getting up for the first time.

Is the faculty of observing on the decline

Yet it appears that scarcely any improvement in the faculty of observing is being made. Vast has been the increase of knowledge in pathology — that science which teaches us the final change produced by disease on the human frame — scarce any in the art of observing the signs of the change while in progress. Or, rather, is it not to be feared that observation, as an essential part of medicine, has been declining?

Which of us has not heard fifty times, from one or another, a nurse, or a friend of the sick, aye, and a medical friend too, the following remark: — "So A is worse, or B is dead. I saw him the day before; I thought him so much better; there certainly was no appearance from which one could have expected so sudden (?) a change." I have never heard anyone say, though one would think it the more natural thing, "There *must* have been *some* appearance, which I should have seen if I had but looked; let me try and remember what there was, that I may observe another time." No, this is not what people say. They boldly assert that there was nothing to observe, not that their observation was at fault.

Let people who have to observe sickness and death look back and try to register in their observation the appearances which have preceded relapse, attack, or death, and not assert that there were none, or that there were not the *right* ones.[xxxvii]

Observation of general conditions

A want of the habit of observing conditions and an inveterate habit of taking averages are each of them often equally misleading.

Men whose profession like that of medical men leads them to observe only, or chiefly, palpable and permanent organic changes are often just as wrong in their opinion of the result as those who do not observe at all. For instance, there is a broken leg; the surgeon has only to look at it once to know; it will not be different if he sees it in the morning to what it would have been had he seen it in the evening. And in whatever conditions the patient is, or is likely to be, there will still be the broken leg, until it is set. The same with many organic diseases. An experienced physician has but to feel the pulse once, and he knows that there is aneurism which will kill some time or other.

But with the great majority of cases, there is nothing of the kind; and the power of forming any correct opinion as to the result must entirely depend upon an enquiry into all the conditions in which the patient lives. In a complicated state of society in large towns, death, as every one of great experience knows, is far less often produced by any one organic disease than by some illness, after many other diseases, producing just the sum of exhaustion necessary for death. There is nothing so absurd, nothing so misleading as the verdict one so often hears: So-and-so has no organic disease, — there is no reason why he should not live to extreme old age; sometimes the clause is added, sometimes not: Provided he has quiet, good food, good air, etc., etc., etc.; the verdict is repeated by ignorant people *without* the latter clause; or there is no possibility of the conditions of the latter clause being obtained; and this, the *only* essential part of the whole, is made of no effect. I have heard a physician, deservedly eminent; assure the friends of a patient of his recovery. Why? Because he had now prescribed a course, every detail of which the patient had followed for years. And because he had forbidden a course which the patient could not by any possibility alter.[xxxviii]

Undoubtedly a person of no scientific knowledge whatever but of observation and experience in these kinds of conditions, will be able to arrive at a much truer guess as to the probable duration of life of members of a family or inmates of a house, than the most scientific physician to whom the same persons are brought to have their pulse felt; no enquiry being made into their conditions.

In Life Insurance and such like societies, were they instead of having the persons examined by a medical man, to have the houses, conditions, ways of life, of these persons examined, at how much truer results would they arrive! W. Smith appears a fine hale man, but it might be known that the next cholera epidemic he runs a bad chance. Mr. and Mrs. J. are a strong healthy couple, but it might be known that they live in such a house, in such a part of London, so near the river that they will kill four-fifths of their children; which of the children will be the ones to survive might also be known.

"Average rate of mortality" tells us only that so many per cent. will die. Observation must tell us *which* in the hundred they will be who will die.

Averages again seduce us away from minute observation. "Average mortalities" merely tell that so many per cent. die in this town and so many in that, per annum. But whether A or B will be among these, the "average rate" of course does not tell. We know, say, that from 22 to 24 per 1,000 will die in London next year. But minute enquiries into conditions enable us to know that in such a district, nay, in such a street,—or even on one side of that street, in such a particular house, or even on one floor of that particular house, will be the excess of mortality, that is, the person will die who ought not to have died before old age.

Now, would it not very materially alter the opinion of whoever were endeavoring to form one, if he knew that from that floor, of that house, of that street the man came?

Much more precise might be our observations even than this and much more correct our conclusions.

It is well known that the same names may be seen constantly recurring on workhouse books for generations. That is, the persons were born and brought up, and will be born and brought up, generation after generation, in the conditions which make paupers. Death and disease are like the workhouse, they take from the same family, the same house, or in other words the same conditions. Why will we not observe what they are?

The close observer may safely predict that such a family, whether its members marry or not, will become extinct; that such another will degenerate morally and physically. But who learns the lesson? On the contrary, it may be well known that the children die in such a house at the rate of 8 out of 10; one would think that nothing more need be said; for how could Providence speak more distinctly? yet nobody listens, the family goes on living there till it dies out, and then some other family takes it. Neither would they listen "if one rose from the dead."

What observation is for

In dwelling upon the vital importance of *sound* observation, it must never be lost sight of what observation is for. It is not for the sake of piling up miscellaneous information or curious facts, but for the sake of saving life and increasing health and comfort. The caution may seem useless, but it is quite surprising how many men (some women do it too), practically behave as if the scientific end were the only one in view, or as if the sick body were but a reservoir for stowing medicines into, and the surgical disease only a curious case the sufferer has made for the attendant's special information. This is really no exaggeration. You think, if you suspected your patient was being poisoned, say, by a copper kettle, you would instantly, as you ought, cut off all possible connection between him and the suspected source of injury, without regard to the fact that a curious mine of observation is thereby lost. But it is not everybody who does so, and it has actually been made a question of medical ethics, what should the medical man do if he suspected poisoning? The answer seems a very simple one, — insist on a confidential nurse being placed with the patient, or give up the case.

What a confidential nurse should be

And remember every nurse should be one who is to be depended upon, in other words, capable of being a "confidential" nurse. She does not know how soon she may find herself placed in such a situation; she must be no gossip, no vain talker; she should never answer questions about her sick except to those who have a right to ask them; she must, I need not say, be strictly sober and honest; but more than this, she must be a religious and devoted woman; she must have a respect for her own calling, because God's precious gift of life is often literally placed in her hands; she must be a sound, and close, and quick observer; and she must be a woman of delicate and decent feeling.

Observation is for practical purposes

To return to the question of what observation is for: — It would really seem as if some had considered it as its own end, as if detection, not cure, was their business; nay more, in a recent celebrated trial, three medical men, according to their own account, suspected poison, prescribed for dysentery, and left the patient to the poisoner. This is an extreme case. But in a small way, the same manner of acting falls under the cognizance of us all. How often the attendants of a case have stated that they knew perfectly well that the patient could not get well in such an air, in such a room, or under such circumstances, yet have gone on dosing him with medicine, and making no effort to remove the poison from him, or him from the poison which they knew was killing him; nay, more, have sometimes not so much as mentioned their conviction in the right quarter — that is, to the only person who could act in the matter.

Conclusion

Sanitary nursing as essential in surgical as in medical cases, but not to supersede surgical nursing

The whole of the preceding remarks apply even more to children and to puerperal women than to patients in general. They also apply to the nursing of surgical, quite as much as to that of medical cases. Indeed, if it be possible, cases of external injury require such care even more than sick. In surgical wards, one duty of every nurse certainly is *prevention*. Fever, or hospital gangrene, or purulent discharge of some kind may else supervene. Has she a case of compound fracture, of amputation, or of erysipelas, it may depend very much on how she looks upon the things enumerated in these notes, whether one or other of these hospital diseases attacks her patient or not. If she allows her ward to become filled with the peculiar close foul smell, so apt to be produced among surgical cases, especially where there is great suppuration and discharge, she may see a vigorous patient in the prime of life gradually sink and die where, according to all human probability, he ought to have recovered. The surgical nurse must be ever on the watch, ever on her guard, against want of cleanliness, foul air, want of light, and of warmth.

Nevertheless let no one think that because *sanitary* nursing is the subject of these notes, therefore, what may be called the handicraft of nursing is to be undervalued. A patient may be left to bleed to death in a sanitary palace. Another who cannot move himself may die of bed-sores, because the nurse does not know how to change and clean him, while he has every requisite of air, light, and quiet. But nursing, as a handicraft, has not been treated of here for three reasons:

1. that these notes do not pretend to be a manual for nursing, any more than for cooking for the sick;

2. that the writer, who has herself seen more of what may be called surgical nursing, *i.e.*, practical manual nursing, than, perhaps, any one in Europe, honestly believes that it is impossible to learn it from any book, and that it can only be thoroughly learnt in the wards of a hospital; and she also honestly believes that the perfection of surgical nursing may be seen practiced by the old-fashioned "Sister" of a London hospital, as it can be seen nowhere else in Europe.

3. While thousands die of foul air, etc., who have this surgical nursing to perfection, the converse is comparatively rare.

Children: their greater susceptibility to the same things

To revert to children. They are much more susceptible than grown people to all noxious influences. They are affected by the same things, but much more quickly and seriously, viz., by want of fresh air, of proper warmth, want of cleanliness in house, clothes, bedding, or body, by startling noises, improper food, or want of punctuality, by dullness and by want of light, by too much or too little covering in bed, or when up, by want of the spirit of management generally in those in charge of them. One can, therefore, only press the importance, as being yet greater in the case of children, greatest in the case of sick children, of attending to these things.

That which, however, above all, is known to injure children seriously is foul air, and most seriously at night. Keeping the rooms where they sleep tight shut up is destruction to them. And, if the child's breathing be disordered by disease, a few hours only of such foul air may endanger its life, even where no inconvenience is felt by grown-up persons in the same room.

The following passages, taken out of an excellent "Lecture on Sudden Death in Infancy and Childhood," just published show the vital importance of careful nursing of children. "In the great majority of instances, when death suddenly befalls the infant or young child, it is an *accident*; it is not a necessary, inevitable result of any disease from which it is suffering."

It may be here added that it would be very desirable to know how often death is, with adults, "not a necessary, inevitable result of any disease." Omit the word "sudden;" (for *sudden* death is comparatively rare in middle age) and the sentence is almost equally true for all ages.

The following causes of "accidental" death in sick children are enumerated: — "Sudden noises, which startle — a rapid change of temperature, which chills the surface, though only for a moment — a rude awakening from sleep — or even an over-hasty, or an over-full meal" — "any sudden impression on the nervous system — any hasty alteration of posture — in short, any cause whatever by which the respiratory process may be disturbed."

It may again be added, that, with very weak adult patients, these causes are also (not often "suddenly fatal," it is true, but) very much oftener than is at all generally known, irreparable in their consequences.

Both for children and for adults, both for sick and for well (although more certainly in the case of sick children than in any others), I would here again repeat, the most frequent and most fatal cause of all is sleeping, for even a few hours, much more for weeks and months, in foul air, a condition which, more than any other condition, disturbs the respiratory process, and tends to produce "accidental" death in disease.

I need hardly here repeat the warning against any confusion of ideas between cold and fresh air. You may chill a patient fatally without giving him fresh air at all.

And you can quite well, nay, much better, give him fresh air without chilling him. This is the test of a good nurse.

In cases of long recurring faintness's from disease, for instance, especially disease which affects the organs of breathing, fresh air to the lungs, warmth to the surface, and often (as soon as the patient can swallow) hot drink, these are the right remedies and the only ones. Yet, oftener than not, you see the nurse or mother just reversing this; shutting up every cranny through which fresh air can enter, and leaving the body cold, or perhaps throwing a greater weight of clothes upon it, when already it is generating too little heat.

"Breathing carefully, anxiously, as though respiration were a function which required all the attention for its performance," is cited as a not unusual state in children, and as one calling for care in all the things enumerated above. That breathing becomes an almost voluntary act, even in grown up patients who are very weak, must often have been remarked.

"Disease having interfered with the perfect accomplishment of the respiratory function, some sudden demand for its complete exercise, issues in the sudden standstill of the whole machinery," is given as one process: — "life goes out for want of nervous power to keep the vital functions in activity," is given as another, by which "accidental" death is most often brought to pass in infancy.

Also in middle age, both these processes may be seen ending in death, although generally not suddenly. And I have seen, even in middle age, the "*sudden* stand-still" here mentioned, and from the same causes.

Summary

To sum up: — the answer to two of the commonest objections urged, one by women themselves, the other by men, against the desirableness of sanitary knowledge for women, *plus* a caution, comprises the whole argument for the art of nursing.

Reckless amateur physicking[14] by women. Real knowledge of the laws of health alone can check this.

(1.) It is often said by men, that it is unwise to teach women anything about these laws of health, because they will take to physicking, — that there is a great deal too much of amateur physicking as it is, which is indeed true. One eminent physician told me that he had known more calomel given, both at a pinch and for a continuance, by mothers, governesses, and nurses, to children than he had ever heard of a physician prescribing in all his experience. Another says that women's only idea in medicine is calomel and aperients. This is undeniably too often the case. There is nothing ever seen in any professional practice like the reckless physicking by amateur females.[xxxix] But this is just what the really experienced and observing nurse does *not* do; she neither physics herself nor others. And to cultivate in things pertaining to health observation and experience in women who are mothers, governesses or nurses, is just the way to do away with amateur physicking, and if the doctors did but know it, to make the nurses obedient to them, — helps to them instead of hindrances. Such education in women would indeed diminish the doctor's work — but no one really believes that doctors wish that there should be more illness, in order to have more work.

---

[14] A medicine or drug, especially a cathartic.

What pathology teaches. What observation alone
teaches. What medicine does. What nature alone does.

(2.) It is often said by women, that they cannot know
anything of the laws of health, or what to do to
preserve their children's health, because they can
know nothing of "Pathology," or cannot "dissect,"
— a confusion of ideas which it is hard to attempt
to disentangle. Pathology teaches the harm that
disease has done. But it teaches nothing more. We
know nothing of the principle of health, the positive
of which pathology is the negative, except from
observation and experience. And nothing but
observation and experience will teach us the ways
to maintain or to bring back the state of health. It is
often thought that medicine is the curative process.
It is no such thing; medicine is the surgery of
functions, as surgery proper is that of limbs and
organs. Neither can do anything but remove
obstructions; neither can cure; nature alone cures.
Surgery removes the bullet out of the limb, which
is an obstruction to cure, but nature heals the
wound. So it is with medicine; the function of an
organ becomes obstructed; medicine, so far as we
know, assists nature to remove the obstruction, but
does nothing more. And what nursing has to do in
either case, is to put the patient in the best condition
for nature to act upon him. Generally, just the
contrary is done. You think fresh air, and quiet and
cleanliness   extravagant,   perhaps   dangerous,
luxuries, which should be given to the patient only
when quite convenient, and medicine the *sine qua
non*, the panacea. If I have succeeded in any
measure in dispelling this illusion, and in showing
what true nursing is, and what it is not, my object
will have been answered.

Now for the caution:—

(3.) It seems a commonly received idea among men and
even among women themselves that it requires
nothing but a disappointment in love, the want of
an object, a general disgust, or incapacity for other
things, to turn a woman into a good nurse.

This reminds one of the parish where a stupid old man
was set to be schoolmaster because he was "past
keeping the pigs."

Apply the above receipt for making a good nurse to
making a good servant. And the receipt will be found to
fail.

Yet popular novelists of recent days have invented
ladies disappointed in love or fresh out of the drawing-
room turning into the war-hospitals to find their
wounded lovers, and when found, forthwith abandoning
their sick-ward for their lover, as might be expected.
Yet in the estimation of the authors, these ladies were
none the worse for that, but on the contrary were
heroines of nursing.

What cruel mistakes are sometimes made by benevolent
men and women in matters of business about which
they can know nothing and think they know a great
deal.

The everyday management of a large ward, let alone of
a hospital — the knowing what are the laws of life and
death for men, and what the laws of health for wards —
(and wards are healthy or unhealthy, mainly according
to the knowledge or ignorance of the nurse) — are not
these matters of sufficient importance and difficulty to
require learning by experience and careful inquiry, just
as much as any other art? They do not come by
inspiration to the lady disappointed in love, nor to the
poor workhouse drudge hard up for a livelihood.

And terrible is the injury which has followed to the sick from such wild notions!

In this respect (and why is it so?), in Roman Catholic countries, both writers and workers are, in theory at least, far before ours. They would never think of such a beginning for a good working Superior or Sister of Charity. And many a Superior has refused to admit a *Postulant* who appeared to have no better "vocation" or reasons for offering herself than these.

It is true *we* make "no vows." But is a "vow" necessary to convince us that the true spirit for learning any art, most especially an art of charity, aright, is not a disgust to everything or something else? Do we really place the love of our kind (and of nursing, as one branch of it,) so low as this? What would the Mère Angélique of Port Royal, what would our own Mrs. Fry have said to this?

Note: — I would earnestly ask my sisters to keep clear of both the jargons now current everywhere (for they *are* equally jargons); of the jargon, namely, about the "rights" of women, which urges women to do all that men do, including the medical and other professions, merely because men do it, and without regard to whether this *is* the best that women can do; and of the jargon which urges women to do nothing that men do, merely because they are women, and should be "recalled to a sense of their duty as women," and because "this is women's work," and "that is men's," and "these are things which women should not do," which is all assertion and nothing more. Surely woman should bring the best she has, *whatever* that is, to the work of God's world, without attending to either of these cries. For what are they, both of them, the one *just* as much as the other, but listening to the "what people will say," to opinion, to the "voices from without?" And as a wise man has said, no one has ever done anything great or useful by listening to the voices from without.

You do not want the effect of your good things to be, "How wonderful for a *woman*!" nor would you be deterred from good things, by hearing it said, "Yes, but she ought not to have done this, because it is not suitable for a woman." But you want to do the thing that is good, whether it is "suitable for a woman" or not.

It does not make a thing good, that it is remarkable that a woman should have been able to do it. Neither does it make a thing bad, which would have been good had a man done it, that it has been done by a woman.

Oh, leave these jargons, and go your way straight to God's work, in simplicity and singleness of heart.

Appendix
Table A. Great Britain: Ages

NURSES.	Nurse (not Domestic Servant)	Nurse (Domestic Servant)
All Ages	25,466	39,139
Under 5 Years.	...	...
5—	...	508
10—	...	7,259
15—	...	10,355
20—	624	6,537
25—	817	4,174
30—	1,118	2,495
35—	1,359	1,681
40—	2,223	1,468
45—	2,748	1,206
50—	3,982	1,196
55—	3,456	833
60—	3,825	712
65—	2,542	369
70—	1,568	204
75—	746	101
80—	311	25
85 and Upwards	147	16

Table B. Aged 20 Years of Age and Upwards

	Nurse (not Domestic Servant)	Nurse (Domestic Servant)
Great Britain and Islands in the British Seas.	25,466	21,017
England and Wales.	23,751	18,945
Scotland.	1,543	1,922
Islands in the British Seas.	172	150
1st Division. London.	7,807	5,061
2nd Division. South Eastern.	2,878	2,514
3rd Division. South Midland.	2,286	1,252
4th Division. Eastern Counties.	2,408	959
5th Division. South Western Counties.	3,055	1,737
6th Division. West Midland Counties.	1,225	2,383
7th Division. North Midland Counties.	1,003	957
8th Division. North Western Counties.	970	2,135
9th Division. Yorkshire.	1,074	1,023
10th Division. Northern Counties.	402	410
11th Division. Monmouth and Wales.	343	614

Note as to the Number of Women employed as Nurses in Great Britain.

25,466 were returned, at the census of 1851, as nurses by profession, 39,139 nurses in domestic service,[xl] and 2,822 midwives. The numbers of different ages are shown in table A, and in table B their distribution over Great Britain.

To increase the efficiency of this class, and to make as many of them as possible the disciples of the true doctrines of health, would be a great national work.

For there the material exists, and will be used for nursing, whether the real "conclusion of the matter" be to nurse or to poison the sick. A man, who stands perhaps at the head of our medical profession, once said to me, I send a nurse into a private family to nurse the sick, but I know that it is only to do them harm.

Now a nurse means any person in charge of the personal health of another. And, in the preceding notes, the term *nurse* is used indiscriminately for amateur and professional nurses. For, besides nurses of the sick and nurses of children, the numbers of whom are here given, there are friends or relations who take temporary charge of a sick person, there are mothers of families. It appears as if these unprofessional nurses were just as much in want of knowledge of the laws of health as professional ones.

Then there are the school-mistresses of all national and other schools throughout the kingdom. How many of children's epidemics originate in these! Then the proportion of girls in these schools, who become mothers or members among the 64,600 nurses recorded above, or schoolmistresses in their turn. If the laws of health, as far as regards fresh air, cleanliness, light, etc., were taught to these, would this not prevent some children being killed, some evil being perpetuated? On women we must depend, first and last, for personal and household hygiene—for preventing the race from degenerating in as far as these things are concerned. Would not the true way of infusing the art of preserving its own health into the human race be to teach the female part of it in schools and hospitals, both by practical teaching and by simple experiments, in as far as these illustrate what may be called the theory of it?

Endnotes

i   Upon this fact the most wonderful deductions have been strung. For a long time an announcement something like the following has been going the round of the papers: — "More than 25,000 children die every year in London under 10 years of age; therefore we want a Children's Hospital." This spring there was a prospectus issued, and divers other means taken to this effect:—"There is a great want of sanitary knowledge in women; therefore we want a Women's Hospital." Now, both the above facts are too sadly true. But what is the deduction? The causes of the enormous child mortality are perfectly well known; they are chiefly want of cleanliness, want of ventilation, want of white-washing; in one word, defective household hygiene. The remedies are just as well known; and among them is certainly not the establishment of a Child's Hospital. This may be a want; just as there may be a want of hospital room for adults. But the Registrar-General would certainly never think of giving us as a cause for the high rate of child mortality in (say) Liverpool that there was not sufficient hospital room for children; nor would he urge upon us, as a remedy, to found a hospital for them.

Again, women, and the best women, are woefully deficient in sanitary knowledge; although it is to women that we must look, first and last, for its application, as far as household hygiene is concerned. But who would ever think of citing the institution of a Women's Hospital as the way to cure this want?

We have it, indeed, upon very high authority that there is some fear lest hospitals, as they have been hitherto, may not have generally increased, rather than diminished, the rate of mortality — especially of child mortality.

ii The common idea as to uninhabited rooms is, that they may safely be left with doors, windows, shutters, and chimney board, all closed — hermetically sealed if possible — to keep out the dust, it is said; and that no harm will happen if the room is but opened a short hour before the inmates are put in. I have often been asked the question for uninhabited rooms — But when ought the windows to be opened? The answer is — When ought they to be shut?

iii It is very desirable that the windows in a sick room should be such as that the patient shall, if he can move about, be able to open and shut them easily himself. In fact the sick room is very seldom kept aired if this is not the case — so very few people have any perception of what is a healthy atmosphere for the sick. The sick man often says, "This room where I spend 22 hours out of the 24 is fresher than the other where I only spend 2. Because here I can manage the windows myself." And is true.

iv Dr. Angus Smith's air test, if it could be made of simpler application, would be invaluable to use in every sleeping and sick room. Just as without the use of a thermometer no nurse should ever put a patient into a bath, so should no nurse, or mother, or superintendent be without the air test in any ward, nursery, or sleeping-room. If the main function of a nurse is to maintain the air within the room as fresh as the air without, without lowering the temperature, then she should always be provided with a thermometer which indicates the temperature, with an air test which indicates the organic matter of the air. But to be used, the latter must be made as simple a little instrument as the former, and both should be self-registering. The senses of nurses and mothers become so dulled to foul air that they are perfectly unconscious of what an atmosphere they have let their children, patients, or charges, sleep in. But if the tell-tale air-test were to exhibit in the morning, both to nurses and patients and to the superior officer going round, what the atmosphere has been during the night, I question if any greater security could be afforded against a recurrence of the misdemeanor.

And oh; the crowded national school! where so many children's epidemics have their origin, what a tale its air-test would tell! We should have parents saying, and saying rightly, "I will not send my child to that school, the air-test stands at 'Horrid.'" And the dormitories of our great boarding schools! Scarlet fever would be no more ascribed to contagion, but to its right cause, the air-test standing at "Foul."

We should hear no longer of "Mysterious Dispensations," and of "Plague and Pestilence," being "in God's hands," when, so far as we know, He has put them into our own. The little air-test would both betray the cause of these "mysterious pestilences," and call upon us to remedy it.

v With private sick, I think, but certainly with hospital sick, the nurse should never be satisfied as to the freshness of their atmosphere, unless she can feel the air gently moving over her face, when still.

But it is often observed that nurses who make the greatest outcry against open windows are those who take the least pains to prevent dangerous draughts. The door of the patients' room or ward *must* sometimes stand open to allow of persons passing in and out, or heavy things being carried in and out. The careful nurse will keep the door shut while she shuts the windows, and then, and not before, set the door open, so that a patient may not be left sitting up in bed, perhaps in a profuse perspiration, directly in the draught between the open door and window. Neither, of course, should a patient, while being washed or in any way exposed, remain in the draught of an open window or door.

vi But never, never should the possession of this indispensable lid confirm you in the abominable practice of letting the chamber utensil remain in a patient's room fill, except once in the 24 hours, *i.e.*, when the bed is made. Yes, impossible as it may appear, I have known the best and most attentive nurses guilty of this; aye, and have known, too, a patient afflicted with severe diarrhea for ten days, and the nurse (a very good one) not know of it, because the chamber utensil (one with a lid) was emptied only once in the 24 hours, and that by the housemaid who came in and made the patient's bed every evening. As well might you have a sewer under the room, or think that in a water closet the plug need be pulled up but once a day. Also take care that your *lid*, as well as your utensil, be always thoroughly rinsed.

If a nurse declines to do these kinds of things for her patient, "because it is not her business," I should say that nursing was not her calling. I have seen surgical "sisters," women whose hands were worth to them two or three guineas a-week, down upon their knees scouring a room or hut, because they thought it otherwise not fit for their patients to go into. I am far from wishing nurses to scour. It is a waste of power. But I do say that these women had the true nurse-calling — the good of their sick first, and second only the consideration what it was their "place" to do — and that women who wait for the housemaid to do this, or for the charwoman to do that, when their patients are suffering, have not the *making* of a nurse in them.

vii The health of carriages, especially close carriages, is not of sufficient universal importance to mention here, otherwise than cursorily. Children, who are always the most delicate test of sanitary conditions, generally cannot enter a close carriage without being sick — and very lucky for them that it is so. A close carriage, with the horse-hair cushions and linings always saturated with organic matter, if to this be added the windows up, is one of the most unhealthy of human receptacles. The idea of taking an airing in it is something preposterous. Dr. Angus Smith has shown that a crowded railway carriage, which goes at the rate of 30 miles an hour, is as unwholesome as the strong smell of a sewer, or as a back yard in one of the most unhealth courts off one of the most unhealthy streets in Manchester.

viii God lays down certain physical laws. Upon His carrying out such laws depends our responsibility (that much abused word), for how could we have any responsibility for actions, the results of which we could not foresee — which would be the case if the carrying out of His laws were *not* certain. Yet we seem to be continually expecting that He will work a miracle — *i.e.* break His own laws expressly to relieve us of responsibility.

ix I must say a word about servants' bedrooms. From the way they are built, but oftener from the way they are kept, and from no intelligent inspection whatever being exercised over them, they are almost invariably dens of foul air, and the "servants' health" suffers in an "unaccountable" (?) way, even in the country. For I am by no means speaking only of London houses, where too often servants are put to live under the ground and over the roof. But in a country "*mansion*," which was really a "mansion," (not after the fashion of advertisements), I have known three maids who slept in the same room ill of scarlet fever. "How catching it is," was of course the remark. One look at the room, one smell of the room, was quite enough. It was no longer "unaccountable." The room was not a small one; it was up stairs, and it had two large windows — but nearly every one of the neglects enumerated above was there.

x Is it not living in a continual mistake to look upon diseases, as we do now, as separate entities, which *must* exist, like cats and dogs? instead of looking upon them as conditions, like a dirty and a clean condition, and just as much under our own control;

or rather as the reactions of kindly nature, against the conditions in which we have placed ourselves.

I was brought up, both by scientific men and ignorant women, distinctly to believe that small-pox, for instance, was a thing of which there was once a first specimen in the world, which went on propagating itself, in a perpetual chain of descent, just as much as that there was a first dog, (or a first pair of dogs), and that small-pox would not begin itself any more than a new dog would begin without there having been a parent dog.

Since then I have seen with my eyes and smelt with my nose small-pox growing up in first specimens, either in close rooms or in overcrowded wards, where it could not by any possibility have been "caught," but must have begun.

Nay, more, I have seen diseases begin, grow up, and pass into one another. Now, dogs do not pass into cats.

I have seen, for instance, with a little overcrowding, continued fever grow up; and with a little more, typhoid fever; and with a little more, typhus, and all in the same ward or hut.

Would it not be far better, truer, and more practical, if we looked upon disease in this light?

For diseases, as all experience shows are adjectives, not noun substantives.

xi   That excellent paper, the Builder, mentions the lingering of the smell of paint for a month about a house as a proof of want of ventilation. Certainly — and, where there are ample windows to open, and these are never opened to get rid of the smell of paint, it is a proof of want of management in using the means of ventilation. Of course the smell will then remain for months. Why should it go?

xii   Why should you let your patient ever be surprised, except by thieves? I do not know. In England, people do not come down the chimney, or through the window, unless they are thieves. They come in by the door, and somebody must open the door to them. The "somebody" charged with opening the door is one of two, three, or at most four persons. Why cannot these, at most, four persons be put in charge as to what is to be done when there is a ring at the door bell?

The sentry at a post is changed much oftener than any servant at a private house or institution can possibly be. But what should we think of such an excuse as this: that the enemy had entered such a post because A and not B had been on guard? Yet I have constantly heard such an excuse made in the private house or institution and accepted: viz., that such a person had been "let in" or *not* "let in," and such a parcel had been wrongly delivered or lost because A and not B had opened the door!

xiii   There are many physical operations where ceteris paribus the danger is in a direct ratio to the time the operation lasts; and ceteris paribus the operator's success will be in direct ratio to his quickness. Now there are many mental operations where exactly the same rule holds good with the sick; ceteris paribus their capability of bearing such operations depends directly on the quickness, without hurry, with which they can be got through.

xiv   So true is this that I could mention two cases of women of very high position, both of whom died in the same way of the consequences of a surgical operation. And in both cases, I was told by the highest authority that the fatal result would not have happened in a London hospital.

What institutions are the exception?

But, as far as regards the art of petty management in hospitals, all the military hospitals I know must be excluded. Upon my own experience I stand, and I solemnly declare that I have seen or know of fatal accidents, such as suicides in *delirium tremens*, bleedings to death, dying patients dragged out of bed by drunken Medical Staff Corps men, and many other things less patent and striking, which would not have happened in London civil hospitals nursed by women. The medical officers should be absolved from all blame in these accidents. How can a medical officer mount guard all day and all night over a patient (say) in *delirium tremens*? The fault lies in there being no organized system of attendance. Were a trustworthy *man* in charge of each ward, or set of wards, not as office clerk, but as head nurse, (and head nurse the best hospital sergeant, or ward master, is not now and cannot be, from default of the proper regulations), the thing would not, in all probability, have happened. But were a trustworthy *woman* in charge of the ward, or set of wards, the thing would not, in all certainty, have happened. In other words, it does not happen where a trustworthy woman is really in charge. And, in these remarks, I by no means refer only to exceptional times of great emergency in war hospitals, but also, and quite as much, to the ordinary run of military hospitals at home, in time of peace; or to a time in war when our army was actually more healthy than at home in peace, and the pressure on our hospitals consequently much less.

Nursing in Regimental Hospitals.

It is often said that, in regimental hospitals, patients ought to "nurse each other," because the number of sick altogether being, say, but thirty, and out of these one only perhaps being seriously ill, and the other twenty-nine having little the matter with them, and nothing to do, they should be set to nurse the one; also, that soldiers are so trained to obey, that they will be the most obedient, and therefore the best of nurses, add to which they are always kind to their comrades.

Now, have those who say this, considered that, in order to obey, you must know *how* to obey, and that these soldiers certainly do not know how to obey in nursing. I have seen these "kind" fellows (and how kind they are no one knows so well as myself) move a comrade so that, in one case at least, the man died in the act. I have seen the comrades' "kindness" produce abundance of spirits, to be drunk in secret. Let no one understand by this that female nurses ought to, or could be introduced in regimental hospitals. It would be most undesirable, even were it not impossible. But the head nurseship of a hospital sergeant is the more essential, the more important, the more inexperienced the nurses. Undoubtedly, a London hospital "sister" does sometimes set relays of patients to watch a critical case; but, undoubtedly also, always under her own superintendence; and she is called to whenever there is something to be done, and she knows how to do it. The patients are not left to do it of their own unassisted genius, however "kind" and willing they may be.

xv Fortunate it is if her skirts do not catch fire — and if the nurse does not give herself up a sacrifice together with her patient, to be burnt in her own petticoats. I wish the Registrar-General would tell us the exact number of deaths by burning occasioned by this absurd and hideous custom. But if people will be stupid, let them take measures to protect themselves from their own stupidity — measures which every chemist knows, such as putting alum into starch, which prevents starched articles of dress from blazing up.

Indecency of the crinolines.

I wish too that people who wear crinoline could see the indecency of their own dress as other people see it. A respectable elderly woman stooping forward, invested in crinoline, exposes quite as much of her own person to the patient lying in the room as any opera-dancer does on the stage. But no one will ever tell her this unpleasant truth.

xvi It is absolutely essential that a nurse should lay this down as a positive rule to herself, never to speak to any patient who is standing or moving, as long as she exercises so little observation as not to know when a patient cannot bear it. I am satisfied that many of the accidents which happen from feeble patients tumbling down stairs, fainting after getting up, &c., happen solely from the nurse popping out of a door to speak to the patient just at that moment; or from his fearing that she will do so. And that if the patient were even left to himself, till he can sit down, such accidents would much seldom occur. If the nurse accompanies the patient let her not call upon him to speak. It is incredible that nurses cannot picture to themselves the strain upon the heart, the lungs, and the brain, which the act of moving is to any feeble patient.

xvii As an old experienced nurse, I do most earnestly deprecate all such careless words. I have known patients delirious all night, after seeing a visitor who called them "better," thought they "only wanted a little amusement," and who came again, saying, "I hope you were not the worse for my visit," neither waiting for an answer, nor even looking at the case. No real patient will ever say, "Yes, but I was a great deal the worse."

It is not, however, either death or delirium of which, in these cases, there is most danger to the patient. Unperceived consequences are far more likely to ensue. *You* will have impunity — the poor patient will *not*. That is, the patient will suffer, although neither he nor the inflictor of the injury will attribute it to its real cause. It will not be directly traceable, except by a very careful observant nurse. The patient will often not even mention what has done him most harm.

xviii Sick children, if not too shy to speak, will always express this wish. They invariably prefer a story to be told to them, rather than read to them.

xix It is a matter of painful wonder to the sick themselves how much painful ideas predominate over pleasurable ones in their impressions; they reason with themselves; they think themselves ungrateful; it is all of no use. The fact is, that these painful impressions are far better dismissed by a real laugh, if you can excite one by books or conversation, than by any direct reasoning; or if the patient is too weak to laugh, some impression from nature is what he wants. I have mentioned the cruelty of letting him stare at a dead wall. In many diseases, especially in convalescence from fever, that wall will appear to make all sorts of faces at him; now flowers never do this. Form, color, will free your patient from his painful ideas better than any argument.

xx   I remember a case in point. A man received an injury to the spine, from an accident, which after a long confinement ended in death. He was a workman — had not in his composition a single grain of what is called "enthusiasm for nature," — but he was desperate to "see once more out of window." His nurse actually got him on her back, and managed to perch him up at the window for an instant, "to see out." The consequence to the poor nurse was a serious illness, which nearly proved fatal. The man never knew it; but a great many other people did. Yet the consequence in none of their minds, so far as I know, was the conviction that the craving for variety in the starving eye, is just as desperate as that for food in the starving stomach, and tempts the famishing creature in either case to steal for its satisfaction. No other word will express it but "desperation." And it sets the seal of ignorance and stupidity just as much on the governors and attendants of the sick if they do not provide the sick-bed with a "view" of some kind, as if they did not provide the hospital with a kitchen.

xxi   No one who has watched the sick can doubt the fact, that some feel stimulus from looking at scarlet flowers, exhaustion from looking at deep blue, etc.

xxii   Why, because the nurse has not got some food to-day which the patient takes, can the patient wait four hours for food to-day, who could not wait two hours yesterday? Yet this is the only logic one generally hears. On the other hand, the other logic, viz., of the nurse giving a patient a thing because she has got it, is equally fatal. If she happens to have fresh jelly, or fresh fruit, she will frequently give it to the patient half-an-hour after his dinner, or at his dinner, when he cannot possibly eat that and the broth too — or worse still leave it by his bed-side till he is so sickened with the sight of it, that he cannot eat it at all.

xxiii In the diseases produced by bad food, such as scorbutic dysentery and diarrhea, the patient's stomach often craves for and digests things, some of which certainly would be laid down in no dietary that ever was invented for sick, and especially not for such sick. These are fruit, pickles, jams, gingerbread, fat of ham or of bacon, suet, cheese, butter, milk. These cases I have seen not by ones, nor by tens, but by hundreds. And the patient's stomach was right and the book was wrong. The articles craved for, in these cases, might have been principally arranged under the two heads of fat and vegetable acids.

There is often a marked difference between men and women in this matter of sick feeding. Women's digestion is generally slower.

xxiv It is made a frequent recommendation to persons about to incur great exhaustion, either from the nature of the service or from their being not in a state fit for it, to eat a piece of bread before they go. I wish the recommenders would themselves try the experiment of substituting a piece of bread for a cup of tea or coffee or beef tea as a refresher. They would find it a very poor comfort. When soldiers have to set out fasting on fatiguing duty, when nurses have to go fasting in to their patients, it is a hot restorative they want, and ought to have, before they go, not a cold bit of bread. And dreadful have been the consequences of neglecting this. If they can take a bit of bread *with* the hot cup of tea, so much the better, but not *instead* of it. The fact that there is more nourishment in bread than in almost anything else has probably induced the mistake. That it is a fatal mistake there is no doubt. It seems, though very little is known on the subject, that what "assimilates" itself directly and with the least trouble of digestion with the human body is the best for the above circumstances. Bread requires two or three processes of assimilation, before it becomes like the human body.

The almost universal testimony of English men and women who have undergone great fatigue, such as riding long journeys without stopping, or sitting up for several nights in succession, is that they could do it best upon an occasional cup of tea — and nothing else.

Let experience, not theory; decide upon this as upon all other things.

xxv   In making coffee, it is absolutely necessary to buy it in the berry and grind it at home. Otherwise you may reckon upon its containing a certain amount of chicory, *at least*. This is not a question of the taste or of the wholesomeness of chicory. It is that chicory has nothing at all of the properties for which you give coffee. And therefore you may as well not give it.

Again, all laundresses, mistresses of dairy-farms, head nurses (I speak of the good old sort only — women who unite a good deal of hard manual labor with the head-work necessary for arranging the day's business, so that none of it shall tread upon the heels of something else) set great value, I have observed, upon having a high-priced tea. This is called extravagant. But these women are "extravagant" in nothing else. And they are right in this. Real tea-leaf tea alone contains the restorative they want; which is not to be found in sloe-leaf tea.

The mistresses of houses, who cannot even go over their own house once a day, are incapable of judging for these women. For they are incapable themselves, to all appearance, of the spirit of arrangement (no small task) necessary for managing a large ward or dairy.

xxvi   I once told a "very good nurse" that the way in which her patient's room was kept was quite enough to account for his sleeplessness; and she answered quite good-humoredly she was not at all surprised at it — as if the state of the room were, like the state of the weather, entirely out of her power. Now in what sense was this woman to be called a "nurse?"

xxvii   For the same reason if, after washing a patient, you must put the same night-dress on him again, always give it a preliminary warm at the fire. The night-gown he has worn must be, to a certain extent, damp. It has now got cold from having been off him for a few minutes. The fire will dry and at the same time air it. This is much more important than with clean things.

xxviii   If you like to clean your furniture by laying out your clean clothes upon your dirty chairs or sofa, this is one way certainly of doing it. Having witnessed the morning process called "tidying the room," for many years, and with ever-increasing astonishment, I can describe what it is. From the chairs, tables, or sofa, upon which the "things" have lain during the night, and which are therefore comparatively clean from dust or blacks, the poor "things" having "caught" it, they are removed to other chairs, tables, sofas, upon which you could write your name with your finger in the dust or blacks. The other side of the "things" is therefore now evenly dirtied or dusted. The housemaid then flaps everything, or some things, not out of her reach, with a thing called a duster — the dust flies up, then re-settles more equally than it lay before the operation. The room has now been "put to rights."

xxix   I am sure that a person who has accustomed her senses to compare atmospheres proper and improper, for the sick and for children, could tell, blindfold, the difference of the air in old painted and in old papered rooms, cæteris paribus. The latter will always be musty, even with all the windows open.

xxx   If you like to wipe your dirty door, or some portion of your dirty wall, by hanging up your clean gown or shawl against it on a peg, this is one way certainly, and the most usual way, and generally the only way of cleaning either door or wall in a bedroom!

xxxi   There are, of course cases, as in first confinements, when an assurance from the doctor or experienced nurse to the frightened suffering woman that there is nothing unusual in her case, that she has nothing to fear but a few hours' pain, may cheer her most effectually. This is advice of quite another order. It is the advice of experience to utter inexperience. But the advice we have been referring to is the advice of inexperience to bitter experience; and, in general, amounts to nothing more than this, that *you* think *I* shall recover from consumption, because somebody knows somebody somewhere who has recovered from fever.

I have heard a doctor condemned whose patient did not, alas! recover, because another doctor's patient of a *different* sex, of a *different* age, recovered from a *different* disease, in a *different* place. Yes, this is really true. If people who make these comparisons did but know (only they do not care to know), the care and preciseness with which such comparisons require to be made, (and are made), in order to be of any value whatever, they would spare their tongues. In comparing the deaths of one hospital with those of another, any statistics are justly considered absolutely valueless which do not give the ages, the sexes, and the diseases of all the cases. It does not seem necessary to mention this. It does not seem necessary to say that there can be no comparison between old men with dropsies and young women with consumptions. Yet the cleverest men and the cleverest women are often heard making such comparisons, ignoring entirely sex, age, disease, place — in fact, *all* the conditions essential to the question. It is the merest *gossip.*

xxxii   A small pet animal is often an excellent companion for the sick, for long chronic cases especially. A pet bird in a cage is sometimes the only pleasure of an invalid confined for years to the same room. If he can feed and clean the animal himself, he ought always to be encouraged to do so.

xxxiii   It is a much more difficult thing to speak the truth than people commonly imagine. There is the want of observation *simple*, and the want of observation *compound*, compounded, that is, with the imaginative faculty. Both may equally intend to speak the truth. The information of the first is simply defective. That of the second is much more dangerous. The first gives, in answer to a question asked about a thing that has been before his eyes perhaps for years, information exceedingly imperfect, or says, he does not know. He has never observed. And people simply think him stupid.

The second has observed just as little, but imagination immediately steps in, and he describes the whole thing from imagination merely, being perfectly convinced all the while that he has seen or heard it; or he will repeat a whole conversation, as if it were information which had been addressed to him; whereas it is merely what he has himself said to somebody else. This is the commonest of all. These people do not even observe that they have *not* observed nor remember that they have forgotten.

Courts of justice seem to think that anybody can speak "the whole truth and nothing but the truth," if he does but intend it. It requires many faculties combined of observation and memory to speak "the whole truth" and to say "nothing but the truth."

"I knows I fibs dreadful: but believe me, Miss, I never finds out I have fibbed until they tells me so," was a remark actually made. It is also one of much more extended application than most people have the least idea of.

Concurrence of testimony, which is so often adduced as final proof, may prove nothing more, as is well known to those accustomed to deal with the unobservant imaginative, than that one person has told his story a great many times.

I have heard thirteen persons "concur" in declaring that a fourteenth, who had never left his bed, went to a distant chapel every morning at seven o'clock.

I have heard persons in perfect good faith declare, that a man came to dine every day at the house where they lived, who had never dined there once; that a person had never taken the sacrament, by whose side they had twice at least knelt at Communion; that but one meal a day came out of a hospital kitchen, which for six weeks they had seen provide from three to five and six meals a day. Such instances might be multiplied *ad infinitum* if necessary.

xxxiv   This is important, because on this depends what the remedy will be. If a patient sleeps two or three hours early in the night, and then does not sleep again at all, ten to one it is not a narcotic he wants, but food or stimulus, or perhaps only warmth. If on the other hand, he is restless and awake all night, and is drowsy in the morning, he probably wants sedatives, either quiet, coolness, or medicine, a lighter diet, or all four. Now the doctor should be told this, or how can he judge what to give?

xxxv   It is commonly supposed that the nurse is there to spare the patient from making physical exertion for himself — I would rather say that she ought to be there to spare him from taking thought for himself. And I am quite sure, that if the patient were spared all thought for himself, and *not* spared all physical exertion, he would be infinitely the gainer. The reverse is generally the case in the private house. In the hospital it is the relief from all anxiety, afforded by the rules of a well-regulated institution, which has often such a beneficial effect upon the patient.

xxxvi   It may be too broad an assertion, and it certainly sounds like a paradox. But I think that in no country are women to be found so deficient in ready and sound observation as in England, while peculiarly capable of being trained to it. The French or Irish woman is too quick of perception to be so sound an observer — the Teuton is too slow to be so ready an observer as the English woman might be. Yet English women lay themselves open to the charge so often made against them by men, viz., that they are not to be trusted in handicrafts to which their strength is quite equal, for want of a practiced and steady observation. In countries where women (with average intelligence certainly not superior to that of Englishwomen) are employed, *e.g.,* in dispensing, men responsible for what these women do (not theorizing about man's and woman's "missions"), have stated that they preferred the service of women to that of men, as being more exact, more careful, and incurring fewer mistakes of inadvertence.

Now certainly Englishwomen are peculiarly capable of attaining to this.

I remember when a child, hearing the story of an accident, related by someone who sent two girls to fetch a "bottle of salvolatile from her room;" "Mary could not stir," she said, "Fanny ran and fetched a bottle that was not salvolatile, and that was not in my room."

Now this sort of thing pursues every one through life. A woman is asked to fetch a large new bound red book, lying on the table by the window, and she fetches five small old boarded brown books lying on the shelf by the fire. And this, though she has "put that room to rights" every day for a month perhaps, and must have observed the books every day, lying in the same places, for a month, if she had any observation.

Habitual observation is the more necessary, when any sudden call arises. If "Fanny" had observed "the bottle of salvolatile" in "the aunt's room," every day she was there, she would more probably have found it when it was suddenly wanted.

There are two causes for these mistakes of inadvertence. 1. A want of ready attention; only part of the request is heard at all. 2. A want of the habit of observation.

To a nurse I would add, take care that you always put the same things in the same places; you don't know how suddenly you may be called on some day to find something, and may not be able to remember in your haste where you yourself had put it, if your memory is not in the habit of seeing the thing there always.

xxxvii It falls to few ever to have had the opportunity of observing the different aspects which the human face puts on at the sudden approach of certain forms of death by violence; and as it is a knowledge of little use I only mention it here as being the most startling example of what I mean. In the nervous temperament the face becomes pale (this is the only *recognized* effect); in the sanguine temperament purple; in the bilious yellow, or every manner of color in patches. Now, it is generally supposed that paleness is the one indication of almost any violent change in the human being, whether from terror, disease, or anything else. There can be no more false observation. Granted, it is the one recognized livery, as I have said — *de rigueur* in novels, but nowhere else.

xxxviii I have known two cases, the one of a man who intentionally and repeatedly displaced a dislocation, and was kept and petted by all the surgeons, the other of one who was pronounced to have nothing the matter with him, there being no organic change perceptible, but who died within the week. In both these cases, it was the nurse who, by accurately pointing out what she had accurately observed, to the doctors, saved the one case from persevering in a fraud, the other from being discharged when actually in a dying state.

I will even go further and say, that in diseases which have their origin in the feeble or irregular action of some function, and not in organic change, it is quite an accident if the doctor who sees the case only once a day, and generally at the same time, can form any but a negative idea of its real condition. In the middle of the day, when such a patient has been refreshed by light and air, by his tea, his beef tea, and his brandy, by hot bottles to his feet, by being washed and by clean linen, you can scarcely believe that he is the same person as lay with a rapid fluttering pulse, with puffed eye-lids, with short breath, cold limbs, and unsteady hands, this morning. Now what is a nurse to do in such a case? Not cry, "Lord bless you, sir, why you'd have thought he were a dying all night." This may be true, but it is not the way to impress with the truth a doctor, more capable of forming a judgment from the facts, if he did but know them, than you are. What he wants is not your opinion, however respectfully given, but your facts. In all diseases it is important, but in diseases which do not run a distinct and fixed course, it is not only important, it is essential that the facts the nurse alone can observe, should be accurately observed, and accurately reported to the doctor.

I must direct the nurse's attention to the extreme variation there is not infrequently in the pulse of such patients during the day. A very common case is this: Between 3 and 4 A.M. the pulse becomes quick, perhaps 130, and so thready it is not like a pulse at all, but like a string vibrating just underneath the skin. After this the patient gets no more sleep. About mid-day the pulse has come down to 80; and though feeble and compressible is a very respectable pulse. At night, if the patient has had a day of excitement, it is almost imperceptible. But, if the patient has had a good day, it is stronger and steadier and not quicker than at mid-day. This is a common history of a common pulse; and others, equally varying during the day, might be given. Now, in inflammation, which may almost always be detected by the pulse, in typhoid fever, which is accompanied by the low pulse that nothing will raise, there is no such great variation. And doctors and nurses become accustomed not to look for it. The doctor indeed cannot. But the variation is in itself an important feature.

Cases like the above often "go off rather suddenly," as it is called, from some trifling ailment of a few days, which just makes up the sum of exhaustion necessary to produce death. And everybody cries, who would have thought it? except the observing nurse, if there is one, who had always expected the exhaustion to come, from which there would be no rally, because she knew the patient had no capital in strength on which to draw, if he failed for a few days to make his barely daily income in sleep and nutrition.

I have often seen really good nurses distressed, because they could not impress the doctor with the real danger of their patient; and quite provoked because the patient "would look," either "so much better" or "so much worse" than he really is "when the doctor was there." The distress is very legitimate, but it generally arises from the nurse not having the power of laying clearly and shortly before the doctor the facts from which she derives her opinion, or from the doctor being hasty and inexperienced, and not capable of eliciting them. A man who really cares for his patients, will soon learn to ask for and appreciate the information of a nurse, who is at once a careful observer and a clear reporter.

xxxix I have known many ladies who, having once obtained a "blue pill" prescription from a physician gave and took it as a common aperient two or three times a week — with what effect may be supposed. In one case I happened to be the person to inform the physician of it, who substituted for the prescription a comparatively harmless aperient pill. The lady came to me and complained that it "did not suit her half so well."

If women will take or give physic, by far the safest plan is to send for "the doctor" every time — for I have known ladies who both gave and took physic, who would not take the pains to learn the names of the commonest medicines, and confounded, *e.g.*, colocynth with colchicum. This *is* playing with sharp edged tools "with a vengeance."

There are excellent women who will write to London to their physician that there is much sickness in their neighborhood in the country, and ask for some prescription from him, which they used to like themselves, and then give it to all their friends and to all their poorer neighbors who will take it. Now, instead of giving medicine, of which you cannot possibly know the exact and proper application, nor all its consequences, would it not be better if you were to persuade and help your poorer neighbors to remove the dung-hill from before the door, to put in a window which opens, or an Arnott's ventilator, or to cleanse and lime-wash the cottages? Of these things the benefits are sure. The benefits of the inexperienced administration of medicines are by no means so sure.

Homeopathy has introduced one essential amelioration in the practice of physic by amateur females; for its rules are excellent, its physicking comparatively harmless — the "globule" is the one grain of folly which appears to be necessary to make any good thing acceptable. Let then women, if they will give medicine, give homeopathic medicine. It won't do any harm.

An almost universal error among women is the supposition that everybody *must* have the bowels opened once in every twenty-four hours or must fly immediately to aperients. The reverse is the conclusion of experience.

This is a doctor's subject, and I will not enter more into it; but will simply repeat, do not go on taking or giving to your children your abominable "courses of aperients," without calling in the doctor.

It is very seldom indeed, that by choosing your diet, you cannot regulate your own bowels; and every woman may watch herself to know what kind of diet will do this; I have known deficiency of meat produce constipation, quite as often as deficiency of vegetables; baker's bread much oftener than either. Homemade brown bread will oftener cure it than anything else.

xl   A curious fact will be shown by Table A, viz., that 18,122 out of 39,139, or nearly one-half of all the nurses, in domestic service, are between 5 and 20 years of age.